UNDISCOVERED COUNTRY

Imagining the World to Come

PETER S. HAWKINS

Seabury Books
NEW YORK

Cover painting: "Winter Radiance" detail, oil on canvas,
   by Henry Molter
Cover design: Stefan Killen
Interior design: Ronda Scullen

Library of Congress Cataloging-in-Publication Data

Hawkins, Peter S.
 Undiscovered country : imagining the world to come / Peter S. Hawkins.
   p. cm.
 Includes bibliographical references.
 ISBN 978-1-59627-107-4 (pbk.)
 1. Future life—Christianity. I. Title.
 BT903.H39 2009
 236'.2—dc22
              2008043754
Seabury Books
445 Fifth Avenue
New York, New York 10016

www.seaburybooks.com

An imprint of Church Publishing Incorporated

5 4 3 2 1

For Gregor Goethals
(1926–2008)

CONTENTS

FOREWORD
Barbara Brown Taylor

The slim book you hold in your hands will lead you places you had never imagined going, from the lowest hell where mortal enemies gnaw each other's flesh for all eternity to the highest heaven where words fail in the presence of the love that moves the sun and stars. To visit these places, you need only trust your guide—not Dante Alighieri but Peter Hawkins—who has devoted so much of his life to *The Divine Comedy* that it is sometimes hard to tell the difference between the two.

Like Dante, Hawkins is a layman, not a cleric, who holds the "good of the intellect" as essential to the voyage of faith. He knows so much and says it so well that many a poor reader will decide it is time to get into better intellectual shape. Words may fail finally to describe the deepest realities of life (and afterlife), but that does not excuse anyone from trying. Pilgrims need strong minds as well as strong hearts and bodies for this journey.

Like Dante, Hawkins also knows the "dark wood" of the world he lives in, including the jungle of the human soul. He can describe Tammy Faye Bakker's last appearance on *Larry King Live* with the same pathos he offers Henry Ward Beecher at that great preacher's trial for adultery in Brooklyn Civil Court in 1875. Nothing human is foreign in this book. Everything has its place in the divine landscape.

Above all, like Dante, Hawkins trusts a God who is rooted in human love even when that love is predictably frail or goes pitifully awry. He is a student of what it means to be "up to love," no matter how painful the lesson, which makes him the best kind of teacher. In the end, I think, that is what drives this book: his wish to teach us that our imagination of the afterlife has power to change our lives now—that we need not wait for heaven (or hell) to let God's light lead us higher up and further into What Is Most Real.

Although this is a book for anyone who wants to go there, it is also aimed at preachers—"professionals of what comes next," he calls us—who are expected to have something to say when people ask us about the undiscovered country of life after death.

He is right about that. When I think of all the things I have been called upon to do as an ordained minister, nothing compares to sitting beside the bed of someone whose breath has begun to rattle, with a room full of loved ones standing around waiting to hear what I will say. That is never the end of it, either. Later the man from the funeral home will come to cover the body with his cheap velvet shroud and take it away, before anyone in the room is ready for him to do that. What will the minister say to ease the leave-taking?

What will the minister say later to the grandchild who wants to know where Poppy has gone, or—different death—to the grieving parent who wants to know if babies stay babies in heaven? Later still there will be a whole church full of people waiting to hear what the preacher has to say about where this dear departed soul has gone. Most will listen carefully, not only because they care about the destination of that soul but because they care about the destination of their own.

"Somebody has to die before the hereafter comes up," Hawkins says early in this book. But death is too late to think about the afterlife, at least for those of us who are called upon to answer the question "What's next?" in public.

One reason I have always found that task difficult is because I have so little to go on. While the Hebrew prophets offer a few descriptions of a banquet that sounds heavenly, the Old Testament stays more interested in life than afterlife. Matthew's very Jewish gospel contains at least five references to some outer darkness where "there shall be wailing and gnashing of teeth," but none of the other gospel writers catches his enthusiasm for it. The New Testament as a whole is full of heaven, without any consensus about what it means. Heaven is where God is. Any questions?

As a preacher wedded to scripture, I have been guilty of saying as little about afterlife as the Bible does. Now, with *Undiscovered Country* as my guide, I remember that scripture is not my only source for imagining heaven, hell, or the purgatory of in-between-ness where love is purified.

I have literature, for one thing. Dante wrote more about hell than Matthew ever dreamed of. When I need a refresher in heaven, I do not go to the book of Revelation. I go to George Herbert's "Love Bade Me Welcome," set to music by Ralph Vaughan Williams. For purgatory, there is an embarrassment of riches: the poetry of Sharon Olds and Mark Strand, the short fiction of Andre Dubus and Flannery O'Connor, the essays of Thomas Lynch and Joan Didion, even the screenplays of Alan Ball and Paul Haggis.

I also have art, history, hymnody, and a little theology. I sing of a heavenly Jerusalem I have never seen, although thanks to the hymn I know the place by heart. I fear the hell of Hieronymous Bosch, praying that God does not take as much pleasure in pain as the artist did. When Gregory of Nyssa writes about purgatory,

I think I could go there. Julian of Norwich and John of the Cross seem already to have been there, describing the territory in ways that cause my teeth to chatter.

By his own example, Peter Hawkins reminds me that I may call upon any of these helpers when it is my turn to answer the question, "What's next?" In this book you will spend time not only with Dante Alighieri but also with Frederick Buechner, Marilynne Robinson, William Shakespeare, and Wallace Stevens among others. Those of us responsible for imagining the undiscovered country need all the help we can get. Whether that help comes from John Donne or Tammy Faye Bakker, wise preachers will not refuse it, for the God who shows up in scripture goes on showing up in the world, in visions both sublime and ridiculous.

Another way of saying this is that wise preachers will not refuse to look to our own lives for intimations of the afterlife, for the God who shows up in scripture goes on showing up in us—in our loves, our fears, our tears, our laughter—in our stubborn hope that one day everything we think we know for sure will pale in the presence of What Is Most Real.

God has apparently entrusted the gospel to preachers of flesh and blood. Preachers who likewise trust the human to bear divine news may, in Shakespeare's words, "speak what we feel, not what we ought to say." This is the heart of the matter, Hawkins says— "to say, and not in a private diary, but in the pulpit," that the deep joy of looking into the face of a loved one "is but the first install-ment of an ultimate face-to-face vision already implicit in the ones we now cherish."

I will not ruin the end of this book for you, but it is not a book about coming up with something to say at funerals. It is book about being "up to love" for anyone brave enough to discover how.

AUTHOR'S PREFACE

I t is a fearsome thing to fall into the hands of a dream come true—in my case, the opportunity to deliver the Lyman Beecher Lectures on Preaching at Yale Divinity School. For over three decades I had listened to other people give it their best. They were princes of the pulpit (along with the occasional princess); colleagues on the Yale faculty; and two very close friends. Would it ever be my turn? And if it were, could I ever hold a candle to that long-ago October afternoon when I was a wet-behind-the ears assistant professor of Religion and Literature and Frederick Buechner was the Lyman Beecher lecturer? For three days running, what became his *Telling the Truth: the Gospel as Tragedy, Comedy & Fairy Tale* took my breath away. Back in 1976, I had never encountered anything like Buechner's freedom with Scripture: the way he imagined a chain-smoking Pilate nervously washing his hands of the whole question of Truth or the ripple effect of laughter when the superannuated Abraham and Sarah got their ridiculous good news.

In addition to performing this kind of biblical midrash, Buechner also interlaced his reading of the Bible with the work of novelists and poets who had provided him with another canon—a highly eclectic literary one. There was Melville and Dostoevsky, Gerard Manley Hopkins and L. Frank Baum, but no one more important than Shakespeare. *King Lear* was Buechner's play of choice and the heart of the matter found in throw-away lines that bring down the bloodied curtain on Act V. These are words spoken by a minor character, one of the few left standing at the play's end: "The weight of this sad time we must obey;/ Speak what we feel, not what we ought to say" (5.3.324–325).

As Buechner received his final round of applause on day three, I left the Divinity School's Marquand Chapel in a daze. Whatever Religion and Literature was supposed to be—and in my first year on the job I didn't quite know—this was surely it: an example to measure myself by no matter what my own version of this hybrid enterprise turned out to be. His Beecher Lectures offered a startling mixture of candor, humor, and passion that struck me not only as what I wanted to hear from a preacher but also what I wanted to develop in my own work.

That work, now three decades in the making, has been primarily literary, not biblical or homiletic; it has also been undertaken as a layman who has spent a lifetime listening to other people's sermons. Because my forays into the pulpit have been only occasional, maybe a few times a year, I've had the luxury of abundant lead time and the pizzazz of what is often a special occasion: I've been spared the roll call of Sundays in ordinary time. Unlike almost all of my nearly 150 Beecher predecessors I have not known the week-by-week experience of a preacher who, whether in season or out, takes up the weight of this sad time, Scripture in hand, to deal with, say, the cursing of the out-of-season fig tree or the weird exemplarity of the Unjust Steward. How do the clergy do it?

Yet, even the occasional preacher knows the pressure of those Saturday nights (another weekend ruined!) when, like the hapless disciples on the Sea of Galilee, the nets have been cast out again and again with nothing to show for it, when the words you have been given to preach suddenly seem empty or (even worse) just plain wrong; when you discover, if truth be told, that you no longer have anything to say and wonder how you ever got caught up in this terrible business in the first place. In the middle of the journey of our life, you're lost. You used to think there was a true way and that you were on it; in part, that blessed assurance was why you dared become a preacher. But now?

Perhaps every Beecher Lecturer has tried to answer this question: what to say now? How does anyone, to quote Second Timothy, "proclaim the message; be persistent whether the time is favorable or unfavorable; convince, rebuke, and encourage, with the utmost patience in teaching" (4:2)? Since 1887 my predecessors have faced this challenge by digging deep into the pockets of their life's work to come up with the best they had to share: what they learned in the long practice of ministry both in and out of the pulpit; what understanding of Scripture or theology they hope may revitalize the preacher's mind and heart; or what particular circumstances of the present day may be worth paying attention to—like Henry Van Dyke's lectures, "The Gospel for an Age of Doubt," delivered way back in 1895, which we now foolishly fantasize as a sepia-toned Age of Faith.

Frederick Buechner challenged us to speak honestly about human experience, not as it might or should be, but as it was. The refusal to "make nice," he argued, was precisely what biblical narrative is all about, with its flawed patriarchs and clueless disciples—the human wreckage that God nonetheless deigns to work with. Such honesty was also the great gift of Shakespeare, who closed *King Lear* with a devastating "never, never, never, never, never!" but not without acknowledging, in the midst of that prolonged cry of negation, that something had also come to life: "the old king, with Cordelia in her beauty dead in his arms, is finally turned into a human being."[1] For Buechner, Shakespeare offered neither sermon illustrations nor homiletic *bons mots*: the Bard was far too slippery to be directly useful. Rather, he was a profile in courage, someone willing to look into the "dark and ambiguous heart of things, which is to say into his own heart and into our hearts, too, and [tell] as close to the whole truth as he is able." Listening to these words, one wanted to go and do likewise.

Thirty years after Buechner left his mark on the Beecher legacy it was my turn. For the invitation to join this tradition I owe a debt of gratitude to the faculty of the Yale Divinity School: to David Kelsey—my once and future colleague—who made the nomination, to Dean Harry Attridge and his assistant, Grace Pauls, who hosted my stay on campus, and to Martin Jean, Director of the Institute of Sacred Music, who convinced me not only to revisit Yale in October 2007 but to rejoin the faculty the following year. Martha Dewey was my companion during the lectureship and augmented the pleasure of those days even as she has enriched my life over the last thirty years. The transformation of the lectures into this small volume happened as the result of the good offices of Cynthia Shattuck, who has always made the potentially fraught author-editor relationship into a marriage of true minds, not to mention an occasion for joy. Indulgent friends did me the honor of reading the manuscript with care: Carl Charlson, Rachel Jacoff, William Sargent, Nancy Vickers, and Diana Wylie. The lion's share of thanks on this score, however, goes to Cristine Hutchison-Jones, who not only holds the line on split infinitives and proper semicolon usage but strengthens an argument by challenging it. Henry Molter's beautiful "Winter Solstice" graces my cover, and I am thankful to him and Cristine for their help with its design. Finally, I dedicate this book to Gregor Goethals, my friend and colleague for many years, whose zest for life and grace in the face of death gave me more than I could say as we faced her end together. *Let light perpetual shine upon her.*

Dress Rehearsal before the Real Production

PROLOGUE

Does anyone even think of the afterlife apart from the experience of loss? My guess is no. The land of the living is so preoccupying that it takes some radical disenchantment to get most of us to entertain anything beyond the here and now. Or, to put it another way, somebody has to die before the hereafter comes up.

This was my case, as I will shortly go on to tell. But there was also another discovery—not a loss but a find—that set me searching out what Hamlet famously refers to as that "undiscover'd country from whose bourn/ No traveler returns" (3.1.79–80). My big find was Dante. Everything I have to say about the afterlife in the chapters that follow has been filtered through my reading of his *Divine Comedy*, which has come to inform not only my professional life but my conversation, my dreams, and inevitably my religion. His is not the only point of view that has shaped my own, but because my connection to both poet and text has been profound—and because no one else has given us more to think about concerning the other world—I have felt free to locate my own exploration of the life to come within his imaginative universe. For this to be useful for my readers, who are not likely to have Dante as a conversation partner, some back story is necessary—a prologue that tells you where I am coming from and what I have found along the way.

My own first encounter with Dante was by no means love at first sight; in fact, it took years to develop. I recall absolutely nothing of the *Inferno* from my freshman exposure and took away precious little from a later reading of the entire poem in translation. (I was making up credits in summer school and somehow thought a "comedy" would make good beach reading.) Despite six hundred years of footnotes—all those foreign names, obscure dates, diagrams—I suspected that there was a good deal less here than met the eye. To put it another way, I was bored.

But late in my graduate career at Yale, at the cajoling of a friend, I attended the first session of a yearlong course in the Italian Department offered by a newcomer to the faculty, John Freccero. The rest is history, or at least my little moment of it. Against all odds—I was neither a trained medievalist nor as yet able to read Italian; in fact, I was only an unregistered auditor of the class—I resolved to devote myself to a poem that seemed not only to include the whole world but to be a world in itself. Nothing else I had encountered in literature seemed as "pressed down and overflowing." The only thing like it in this regard was Scripture.

I still wonder how I was suddenly found by a book and what accounted for so dramatic a turn from indifference to passion. It mattered, no doubt, that I had a superb teacher, and also brilliant classmates who later became colleagues and fellow travelers through the labyrinthine ways of professional Dante studies. Then there was the poet's vivid, unconventional presentation of the Christian tradition at a time when I was looking for a more compelling experience of faith than I'd known. Most of all, at a point in my life when I was deeply in love and trying to understand the larger ramifications of my Eros, I found a story of a God rooted in human love.

Over the years my relationship both to poem and poet has evolved. Child of my age, I have inevitably taken on a "hermeneutics of suspicion": the *Comedy*, for all its amazing inner coherence, seems less air-tight. It appears to me not so much a miracle as a stunning achievement. Yet this critical distance has in no way diminished my love for the text. Where it is less air-tight, there is more room to breathe. And the more human that Dante becomes, the more astonishing appears the divinity he is able to suggest within and between his gorgeous lines.

Dante Alighieri was a passionate Christian from the late thirteenth century who had a burden for truth-telling, an evangelical zeal. As a medieval layman, however, he had no pulpit to speak from. Instead, his sermon to the world took the form of a one-hundred-canto poem composed of over fourteen thousand lines, all of it written in a Florentine vernacular that eventually became (and no small thanks to him) Italian. Done in by politics at the age of thirty-six, he was exiled for the rest of his days from a city that would always remain the center of his universe. From the shambles of his life he felt called to speak the word of the Lord like a prophet or apostle, to write something like a Third Testament for his own time and place that would, like Scripture, "convince, rebuke, and encourage."

The great Franciscan and Dominican preachers of his age took up this task in their way; theologians like Bonaventure or Aquinas pursued it in another. Dante learned from and echoed both — the apocalyptic thundering of Petrus Johannis Olivi in Florence's Church of Santa Croce and the theological fastidiousness of St. Thomas in the *Summa theologiae*. Although surrounded by clergy, monastics, and their institutions, he had no ordination other than his baptism, no theological education beyond the one he found for himself. Furthermore, Dante was first and foremost a poet and (as one untimely born) determined to write an epic narrative in verse, a monumental work that would turn his personal exile into an Exodus that could be shared by anyone. To do this, he would trace his spiritual journey onto a typological map that moved from his own personal Egypt to the promised land of God's presence.

Genuine piety aside, however there can be no mistaking Dante's titanic literary ambition in this enterprise. He set out to outshine the masters of antiquity, not to mention every vernacular poet of his own day. Nonetheless, this was poetry with a purpose. As he wrote to his patron Can Grande della Scala, "the aim of the whole as of the part is to remove those living in this life from a state of misery and to lead them to the state of happiness."[2]

To do this—and to suggest the urgent crisis of his times and his singular call to address it—he reached out to "those living in this life" by setting his story in a medieval Christian afterlife consisting of a subterranean hell, a purgatory of uncertain location, and a paradise above the heavens. Conjuring these worlds as no one had before, Dante offered the perspective of eternity, a God's-eye view of humankind, where all hearts were open, all desires known, and no secrets hid. To intensify the connection with his readers, he wrote not in the Latin of the church but in the language of his own corner of the world. He also made himself the protagonist of his own story: a man looking back on the journey of transformation he himself had taken. In this he chose an autobiographical technique he might well have learned from St. Augustine in the *Confessions*, whose mature Christian self, the Bishop of Hippo, recollects his fretful, circuitous movement toward God—the One who, from the very beginning of Augustine's life, had been making mysterious moves on him.

In addition to the man who wrote the poem, there are two other Dantes. The one who tells the tale and occasionally addresses us collectively as *lettore*, "Reader," is referred to by critics as the poet. He is the figure who survives the experience of hell, purgatory, and paradise and then is commissioned by heaven to write the account of his experience "for the good of the world that lives ill" (*Purg.* 32.103).[3] One might also think of him as Dante the preacher, although the author of the *Comedy* speaks through many other characters as well. Finally, there is the terrified figure we meet in the opening canto of *Inferno*, thrashing through the spiritual morass of a "dark wood" which represents at once his own sinfulness and that of the world in which he lives. He is commonly known as the pilgrim. It is in his uncertain footsteps that we make our way.

Although we are instructed by the poet, who has developed an eye for eternity over the course of his remembered journey, it is with the often obtuse pilgrim that we identify. He is the quaking reed who appears to be what most of us are much of the time, and always at the terrible turning points of our lives—someone lost. We recognize his desperation. After all, who, reaching the midpoint of humanity's threescore-and-ten, does not know the panic of everything suddenly coming undone, does not realize that the old tricks no longer work and something terrifyingly new must take their place?

We also catch the poignancy of his situation in the poem's prologue scene: though lost in a dark wood, he sees a mountain aglow with light at its summit. Everything in the pilgrim wants to climb upward to that radiance; yet he cannot do so. In the words of the Book of Common Prayer, he does not have it of himself to help himself; there is very little health in him. In fact, even though heaven is his goal, he soon learns from Virgil, the first of his guides, that the only way to ascend toward the light is through a gradual immersion in darkness. For the sake of his individual salvation as well as for that of the larger social order, he must experience what it is like to live apart from God, in a world without grace and therefore without hope. To understand this, he must go to hell, and for over thirty cantos of the *Inferno* the poet makes us go with him.

As we begin to explore Dante's *Comedy* and learn what it has to tell us about our own present, we need to keep in mind the obvious, the chasm that lies between his age and ours. The world of the poem—both the period it was written in and the literary cosmos it constructs—is not our own. Dante wrote at a time, for instance, when thinking about the afterlife was a preoccupation—and not only a preparation for the future but a way to orient oneself in the here and now. Eternity loomed large, and the way one would spend it depended on choices made in the flesh. Paradoxically, the urgency of the life to come made this mortal life of utmost importance. The church did everything it could to keep the "four last things" urgently alive in the imagination: Death, Judgment, Hell, and Heaven. The day of reckoning, which is projected into the end of time and yet as close to hand as one's own death, was everywhere writ large in paint, sculpture, and stained glass. In countless Last Judgment scenes a Christ in majesty separates sheep from goats. The dead rise up from their graves, Michael the archangel weighs souls in a golden balance, and the damned go to their hideous ruin as the blessed are caught up into bliss.

For centuries interest in this prospect remained vital, fueled not only by Catholic art of the Last Judgment but by Protestant sermons preached in white clapboard meeting houses and along the sawdust trail. Traces of that tradition remained even in my childhood, which otherwise did not include either fear of the lake of fire or anticipation of angels' wings. I was not brought up to think about life beyond the grave, and yet, like many of my generation,

I was raised by parents who decided that a bath, bedtime story, and goodnight kiss were not enough to end the day. There needed to be a prayer. Unwittingly they kept in circulation the ultimate concerns of the late seventeenth-century *New England Primer*, turning each night's going to bed into a preparation for not waking up in the morning:

Now I lay me down to sleep,
I pray the Lord my soul to keep;
and if I die before I wake,
I pray the Lord my soul to take.

Reciting this petition, which is forever lodged in memory, might well have brought on nightmares of extinction. On the contrary, it helped me feel prepared.

But prepared for what? Where precisely was the Lord going to take my soul, and where were all of us going? This is what I wanted to know when, without warning, *she* disappeared. One day, the octogenarian lady who bore my father during the reign of Edward VII, wore hats with plumage and made the sweetest tea, was suddenly no longer at the door of our apartment at mid-afternoon, ready to play. With my father on business in England and my mother left to cope alone, the fact of my adored Grandma's death was judged to be too much for me to bear. (I was only three.) But something had to be said. I kept asking where she was, kept looking in all the places where she used to go when we played hide and seek. My family's solution was to take me out on the apartment house fire escape at nightfall and turn me toward the brightest star in the evening firmament. *That's* where she was now, with God, and twinkling down her love for me from her new home in heaven. I no longer had to hunt for her in closets or behind the sofa. Anytime I wanted to visit, all I had to do was wait for evening. She was only a star away.

Inevitably, there comes a time to put away childish things, and Grandma as celestial constellation was one of them. No more twinkling stars. Heaven itself began to seem suspect. Not that I actively disbelieved what the Creed speaks of as the "life of the world to come." Who wouldn't want more life or another try at a world, especially if it meant being "embraced by the light," as one heard about from countless Near Death Experiences that flood our allegedly secular age? What was promised in church, however, was never spelled out. On the contrary, the souls of the faithful were lost in the abstractions of "joy and felicity," everyone somehow at God's right hand where "there is pleasure for evermore." So the Book of Common Prayer has it when, at the graveside, the priest does his or her best with what is essentially carte blanche — a destination that doesn't seem specific enough to warrant a single Michelin star.

The 1980s and early '90s turned out to be a prolonged putting away of childish things, a drawn out *momento mori*. The church bells of my parish in New York's West Village tolled for a generation of gay men and provided the rest of us with a lifetime's worth of graveside assurances. AIDS cut through my world like a scythe. Oddly, my reliance on the church increased even as I wavered in my thinking about a providence that allegedly shapes our end. The Burial of the Dead in particular cast a much-appreciated sober light and, in its lack of sentimentality, made living through those days easier simply by telling truth. "You are dust, and to dust you shall return." "In the midst of life we are in death."

No one I knew spoke of hell, although elsewhere there were certainly voices screaming hatred and calculating the wages of sin. The default assumption was that some sort of heaven awaited us all. But was there anything more that could be said? Scripture is surprisingly reticent on the matter. There is Paul on the Resurrection body, Jesus on the many mansions of the Father's house, the psychedelic throne room of Revelation and its cubed jewel box of a city in which every tear is washed away. Little enough to go on. Moreover, the last thing I wanted at the time was theological discourse or any attempt at the picture perfect. Perhaps I was overtaken by a cranky refusal to be comforted. The efforts to do so—and in this regard "sympathy" cards were the worst offenders—seemed cheap and offensive.

Then there was *Longtime Companion*, the 1990 film that coincided with the AIDS-related death of my thirty-five-year-old partner. I felt at first as if I had been given a gift when the movie's climactic funeral scene turned out to have been filmed in my New York parish, in the same sanctuary where Luis had been welcomed (on the basis of my faith, not his own) as a lamb of God's flock. "Receive him into the arms of your mercy," the priest had said, "into the blessed rest of everlasting peace, and into the glorious company of the saints in light."

Consoling it was, and yet, as opposed to everyone around me in the theater, I utterly rejected the final scene with its New Age vision of a Fire Island reunion of the living and the dead. Talk about childish things! There was not a dry eye in the house when the credits rolled except for my own. Let's face it, I felt like saying, our beloveds are *not* going to rise from the dunes and, looking fabulous, rush into our open arms at water's edge. I could not bear the sentimentality of it all. Hadn't everything irrevocably changed? To resist the fact that it had, that the dead as we knew them in all the old familiar places were gone, was just fantasy. I wanted nothing to do with it.

Then why, more than twenty years later, did I choose to make my Beecher Lectures and now this book into a meditation on the world to come? Perhaps it is because I am no longer angry, perhaps because I have reached a certain age. There are now so many people I have known, to recall Henry Vaughan's poem, who have crossed over into that "great Ring of pure and endless light."[4] Or, to speak more modestly, so many of my people have died. They remain vivid to me, no matter how minor a part they may have played in my life. They are alive in my dreams or waking thoughts, appearing unexpectedly in my conversation or as an anecdote when I teach. Because they are in my world, might I be part of theirs as well?

And then, to return to my opener, there is the occupational hazard of being a Dante scholar who regularly takes his unsuspecting students on a journey through hell, purgatory, and heaven. Other writers and artists, of course, have explored this territory but, without a doubt, Dante has a corner on the afterlife. No one before or since has mapped the world to come so extensively, in such detail, or with such brilliance. Nor has anyone else forced his readers to consider their present lives from an eternal perspective to such a degree. Thinking about the Four Last Things, imagining what kinds of world might grow out of this one, have become part of the way I live and move and have my being. My studies have rubbed off on me.

Not that you need to be a professional medievalist, with one foot in another age, to take these matters seriously. They are as available as the tabloids we glance at while waiting on line in the supermarket, as cover stories in *Time* and *Newsweek*, or as Barbara Walters TV specials. The Internet hums with Web sites, blogs, and chat rooms that are abuzz with speculation about the beyond. Careers are being built, not to mention fortunes made, by folks like Bill Weise writing about *23 Minutes in Hell* and Don Piper with *90 Minutes in Heaven*. Eschatology fuels the Halloween "Hell

House" phenomenon meant to scare teenagers into the arms of the Lord. It keeps Tim LaHaye's *Left Behind* novels and films in circulation; it motivates legions of Jehovah's Witnesses and Mormon missionaries to pound the pavement day in and day out. There is also the more mainstream evangelical—and immensely successful— *Purpose Driven Life*, whose author's commitment to the afterlife, if down-played in the book as a whole, is nonetheless foundational:

> Life on earth is just the dress rehearsal before the real production. You will spend more time on the other side of death—*in eternity*—than you will here. Earth is the staging area, the preschool, the tryout for your life in eternity. It is the practice workout before the actual game; the warm-up lap before the race begins. This life is the preparation for the next.

Rick Warren's metaphors are a little athletic for the Church Fathers but are of a piece with what they, and indeed Dante, assume. Unlike his forebears, however, Warren does not try to tell what eye has not seen nor ear heard: "It would be like trying to describe the Internet to an ant."[5]

There are a cloud of afterlife witnesses, in other words, both ancient and modern. Although Dante is given pride of place in what follows, he is one among many others I have been drawn to: Augustine and Aquinas, John Donne and Henry Ward Beecher, Frederick Buechner. *Hamlet* keeps on cropping up, along with Emily Dickinson, Gerard Manley Hopkins, and Wallace Stevens. It should be clear from the inclusion of Dickinson and Stevens that I am not interested only in the blessed assurance of those who are of firm convictions—faithful experts of the unknowable. In fact, I am writing primarily for those like myself who are shaky on the existence of any world to come, and convinced that, whatever such a future might turn out to be, it is *terra* absolutely *incognita* for us now—an "undiscover'd country." Hamlet's contemplation of such a destination rose out of terror. The "country" on the other side of our last breath was a hideous prospect, and the "dread of something after death" kept us from murder or suicide—kept us smarting under "the whips and scorns of time." But terror need not be our only anticipation, as human history—and two-thirds of the *Commedia*—bear ample witness. I can imagine the last adventure as the greatest one, a looking forward to what is undiscovered and unknown.

Those who stand firm in the sure and present hope of the resurrection know where they are going. They have what they need and will probably have no use for all my tentative intuitions and guesses, hunches and dreams. For many of the rest of us, on the other hand, any affirmation of the life of the world to come is probably going to be provisional. It will be a faithful leap into the dark, an exercise (though not merely so) in wishful thinking. The "undiscover'd country," in other words, can be mapped not by sight or with certainty but by theological imagination. It is glimpsed with what Scripture refers to as the "eyes of the heart."

So, what *if* we should die before we wake? No one can say for sure what is next. But asking the question need not be an exercise in futility. Indeed, as I hope to demonstrate in the chapters that follow, it can open up worlds of possibility and even make a difference in the way we live now.

No Worst,
There Is None

HELL

C hristianity has been in love with hell for a very long time.
For this fact Scripture alone cannot be held responsible:
despite centuries of Bible thumping and proof tex-
ting, there is actually little to go on. The Hebrew Bible basically
leaves us with a shadowy Sheol to which everyone, the just and
the unjust, descends. Notions of a double resurrection—"some to
everlasting life, and some to shame and everlasting contempt" (Dan
12:2)—develop only late in the formation of the Jewish scriptures,
two centuries before the Common Era. The New Testament writings have more to say about an afterlife, although largely in figura-
tive language when Jesus is speaking in parables or in a prophetic
discourse that is impossible to pin down. Paul's epistles are the ear-
liest Christian writings, dating from the middle of the first century.
He mentions Hades only once, and then in the context of the grave
being swallowed up in resurrection's victory (1 Cor 15:54–55).
The Gospel of John is similarly reserved on the subject.

The picture changes, however, with Mark, Matthew, and Luke,
called the Synoptic Gospels because of their shared resources and
point of view. In their pages, in a few memorable passages, we hear

about a place of punishment called Gehenna where fire burns and the worm carries on its torments forever. In an end time prophecy forecasting when the Son of Man is to come again and take his throne in glory, Matthew's Jesus gives the basic ingredients of the Last Judgment scene that would become so prominent in Christian art: the division of humanity into sheep and goats, the sheep destined for a kingdom prepared for them before the foundation of the world, the goats "for the eternal fire prepared for the devil and his angels" (25:41).

At the conclusion of the New Testament canon, and thus accorded the Bible's resonant last word, is the Revelation according to St. John. It expounds on this eternal division, showing a bejeweled city of light on the one hand, a lake of sulfur and flames on the other. A rich apocalyptic literature followed in Revelation's wake. There are afterlife visions dating from the early centuries of the Common Era and attributed to Peter and Paul; these are followed throughout the Middle Ages by myriad accounts written in the names of saints, popes, monks, and lay people. In these works the fate of the damned burns brightest and for the greatest number of pages. Most often heaven is a radiant moment coming at the end of the tale; purgatory, if mentioned at all in the medieval texts, a mere flash. One wonders why the tradition chose to so accentuate the negative. Perhaps, contrary to the old saying, it was thought that more flies could be caught by vinegar than by honey, more souls saved by the fire and worms than by Jerusalem, our happy home.

Whatever power this fixation on damnation has had over Christian history — frightening the young and inspiring many a disabused grown-up to reject it all as hateful mind control — I am one of those who somehow never heard the call to flee from the wrath to come. In all my years of church-going, no preacher ever strong-armed me into repentance, challenged me to consider my eternal damnation or, so to speak, gave me hell. Was I lucky in this regard, or a willfully selective listener, or just plain hard of heart? It is true that my older brother was temporarily born-again, and with his dramatic turnaround from hoodlum to straight-A student developed a concern for the family's salvation. This was challenging: as a chronically well-behaved, eager-to-please little boy, I struggled with his emphasis on sin—mine in particular. How could I possibly acknowledge myself to be the worst of all sinners when I had so many Sunday School pins to show for my righteousness; when I was, well, so *good*? In fact, the "furnace of fire, where there will be weeping and gnashing of teeth" (Matt 13:42) seemed impossible as a destination for anyone I knew, and after a time my brother's concerns about such things waned.

As a result, hellfire and brimstone held no lasting place in my youth, at a time when one is most vulnerable to being frightened— and manipulated—by religion. (*"Give me a child at an impressionable age* and she is mine for life," said the Scots Presbyterian Miss Jean Brodie in an echo of a famous Jesuit adage.) Instead, my contact was vicarious and literary. First, in an American literature anthology, there was Jonathan Edwards' notorious "Sinners in the Hands of an Angry God" warning the unconverted hearts of mid-eighteenth-century Enfield, Connecticut, that they are right now, though in perfect health and the pride of life, suspended "over the pit of hell, much as one holds a spider, or some loathsome insect over the fire," and hanging there by the slenderest of threads. In another sermon, "Heaven, a World of Love," Edwards is winsome, his vision of beatitude quite beautiful. Nonetheless, he turns in the end to "that dark world" where the Lord "exercises no love, and extends no mercy to any one object there, but pours out upon them horrors without mixture." It may seem to be a very strange "world of love" that requires this dark corollary, but here Edwards was working in a tradition that long preceded him and that spans denominational divides. The *Inferno's* Gates of Hell, before which Dante's damned souls famously abandon hope, also proclaim that the place of eternal suffering was made by "PRIMO AMORE" (3.6), God's primal love. When it came to the pairing of hell and heaven, Edwards was a medieval Catholic.

Later in my afterlife education came James Joyce, from whom I received a Roman Catholic version of hell-raising. In *Portrait of the Artist as a Young Man* Stephen Daedalus and his classmates are given a chapel retreat on the traditional "Four Last Things"; as usual, a great deal more attention is paid to the first three, Death, Judgment, and Hell, than to the fourth, Heaven. The Jesuit retreat master, Father Arnall, first addresses his "dear little brothers in Christ" with a text wrested from Isaiah 5:14: "Therefore Sheol has enlarged its appetite and opened its mouth beyond measure." Schooled in the meditative technique of Ignatius Loyola, the priest begins with an imaginative "composition of place." With rhetorical flourish he takes his impressionable lads where they are very likely to end up should his preaching not have its desired effect. What they are asked to see in their mind's eye is that hell's fire gives off no light but rather "burns eternally in darkness." He wants them to know that the "sickening stench" of this dark prison house "is multiplied a million fold and a million fold again from the millions upon millions of rotting carcasses massed together in the rotting darkness, a huge and rotting human fungus." Father Arnall then goes on to imagine the varied torments, the anguished company of the damned, and the onslaught of demons in their relentless psychological warfare. Particularly terrifying is the punishing voice of conscience now attended to, world without end, too late: "Why did you sin? Why did you turn aside from your pious practices and good works? Why did you not repent your evil ways and turn to God who only waited for your repentance to absolve you of all your sins?"[6]

All of this admonition takes place on day one, at the end of which (at least for this reader) there is nothing more to be said. Yet on the morrow Father Arnall marshals his adolescent charges for more, this time fuelled by Psalm 31:22: "I am driven far from your sight." The priest puts aside the "composition of place" strategy in order to consider the multiple ways the damned come to experience the pain of eternal loss. In the end, however, he nails his argument with an aural fantasy: hell is a vast dark hall utterly silent but for the ticking of a great unseen clock. Over and over it seems to repeat the same two words: *ever, never . . . ever, never.* "Ever to be in hell, never to be in heaven; ever to be shut off from the presence of God, never to enjoy the beatific vision; ever to be eaten with flames, gnawed by vermin, goaded with burning spikes, never to be free from those pains."[7] It comes as no surprise that, though scared half to death in the course of the retreat, Stephen Daedalus eventually runs for his life—out of the world of the church. Given the chance, who would hesitate to follow him out the door?

Certainly not the famous preacher and public figure Henry Ward Beecher, who took flight from all notions of hell and in this regard, as in so many others, stood at the vanguard of changing religious sensibilities in post-Civil War America. It is easy to see his aversion as a reaction to his father, the Reverend Lyman Beecher, for whom hell was a preoccupation. Lyman fretted continually not only about the salvation of his Litchfield, Connecticut congregation—"so many immortal souls are sleeping on the brink of hell"—but over the fact that not one of his many offspring seemed prepared to meet their Maker. "Their whole eternal existence," he lamented in his autobiography, "is every moment liable to become an existence of unchangeable sinfulness and woe." In their youth none of the Beecher children—an extraordinary brood, it turned out—escaped this fear. We see this in the very first entry in Henry's high school journal ("filled mostly with doodles, bits of homework, pithy sayings and the name, 'Nancy' scribbled over and over again in dreamy loops of ink"), which nevertheless shows him suffering from his father's consternation over Last Things: "I prove first that there must be a hell, and then it will appear evident that there must be a judgment."[8]

In time, however, this Calvinist orthodoxy would be jettisoned not only by liberal pastors like Henry Ward Beecher but by the middle class urbanites that made up his Brooklyn congregation. Plymouth Church was arguably the first American "megachurch," a wide open door that, thanks to the pastor's eloquence, drew its congregation from all over Brooklyn and Manhattan as well as from farther afield. Walt Whitman came to hear for himself "the most famous man in America," as did Mark Twain and Abraham Lincoln. Beecher rejected the old-fashioned evangelical fervor of the two Great Awakenings; in its place, he offered a "new age" spirituality of love and acceptance as the religion of the implacable Father gave way to that of a forgiving Son. In the name of love Beecher threw aside not only a reading of Scripture that mistook the metaphorical for the literal, but such cornerstone Calvinist doctrines as original sin, total depravity, and predestination. Twice on Sundays and then again at midweek people listened to the preacher transform their hard-line Protestant heritage with a new kind of feeling-based fervor; they could also read him in the leading newspapers of the day. As Beecher wrote in a *New York Times* column, with a candor that later brought him before ecclesiastical councils, "If I thought that God stood at the door where men go out of life ready to send them down to eternal punishment, my soul would cry out, 'Let there be no god!' My instinct would say, 'Annihilate him!' "

Strong words from a member of America's new religious establishment! Beecher loved to capture attention, to pull out all the stops. But I suspect that there was more than showmanship at stake here. No doubt because of his own strenuous religious upbringing, he was sincerely moved by those parishioners who still lived burdened by religious anxiety: "There are those who will not come into God's kingdom unless they come as Dante went to paradise — by going through hell."[9] He, on the contrary, wanted to spare them fear about the "great furnace of wrath," wanted to lead them into an awareness of a divine love "that sacrifices itself for the good of those who err, and that is as patient with them as a mother is with a sick child." Calling himself a lover of mankind, Beecher even went so far as to repudiate his own religious tradition, insisting, "John Calvin can take care of himself." It was time to stop misrepresenting God by preaching salvation through the threat of damnation. It was time to wake up to God's mercy.

Speaking with his customary theatricality from the stage-like platform of Plymouth Church, Beecher told his flock, "To tell me that at the back of Christ is a God who for unnumbered centuries has gone on creating men and sweeping them like dead flies — nay, like living ones — into hell, is to ask me to worship a being much worse than the conception of any medieval devil as can be imagined." On another occasion he asked his congregation to recall Michelangelo's painting of the Last Judgment, not to savor it as an artistic masterpiece but in order to break its spell — the hold of hell on their imaginations:

> Look at the lower parts of the picture, where with pitch-
> forks men are by devils being cast into cauldrons and into

burning fires, where hateful fiends are gnawing at the skulls of suffering sinners, and where there is hellish cannibalism going on. Let a man look at that picture and the scenes which it depicts, and he sees what were the ideas which men once had of Hell and of divine justice. It was a nightmare as hideous as was ever begotten by the hellish brood itself; and it was an atrocious slander on God . . . I do not wonder that men have reacted from these horrors—I honor them for it.[10]

The arch-villain Beecher is really calling into account here is not Michelangelo but Dante—the particular "medieval devil" who provided the painter (not to mention subsequent Western culture) with a surfeit of pitchforks, cauldrons, and fiends gnawing at the heads of suffering sinners. Long before the Last Judgment adorned the east end of the Sistine Chapel, Dante's *Inferno* was already in wide circulation: copied, illustrated, commented on, and even performed in the streets. (In a tribute to his influence, in fact, Michelangelo includes the poet in his fresco—looking at the damned but positioned safely among the blessed.) It is true that the *Comedy*'s pilgrim only starts his journey in hell and has paradise as his ultimate destination, yet from the very beginning it is the poem's opening installment that has always captured and held popular attention. Today, even passing reference to Dante's "dolorous kingdom" (*Inf.* 34.28) serves as evil's gold standard, as convenient shorthand for denoting the unspeakable: "This is a tale of horrors," says the chief prosecutor of a UN court commenting on the intractable war in Sierra Leone; it moves "beyond the Gothic and into the realm of Dante's *Inferno*."

Where did the poet's vision of damnation come from? Like the folks on the Internet who share their "23 Minutes in Hell" in order to put the fear of God into all who hear them, Dante also claimed personal experience—in his case, not a rapture or out-of-body experience but an actual journey in the flesh. Some of his contemporaries took him at his poem's word. In Boccaccio's mid-fourteenth century biography of the poet we are told that some credulous ladies in Verona, where Dante spent two periods during his exile, crossed to the other side of the street when they saw him coming. They wanted to avoid the man whose grave mien and dark complexion were caused by the heat and smoke of Hades: "Do you see the man who goes down to Hell, and comes again at his pleasure, and brings tidings of them that be below?"[11]

Gullible readers and poetic license aside, we are on surer footing when it comes to thinking about the literary sources Dante may have drawn on. These include the medieval Christian visions of the afterlife mentioned above, which pick up where the sparse and scattered references of Scripture leave off. As the genre developed in the Middle Ages, these works offered him a more and more detailed mapping of the afterlife, as well as some of the elements he would take up and transform. More influential, however, was the *Aeneid*, the pre-Christian text without which the *Divine Comedy* is unimaginable—and not only because Virgil, its author, is the pilgrim's guide for two-thirds of the way. The sixth book of the *Aeneid* is particularly important, with its account of the hero's descent to the world of the dead in order to receive his transforming vision of the future. Aeneas eventually receives this forecast in the Elysian Fields, which is as close as the ancient Roman world came to imagining what heaven might be like. On his way there the Sibyl, his guide, describes another realm they are *not* meant to enter but only to take into account. This is Tartarus, the antithesis of Elysium, an iron-walled city locked tight against all comers. In it the unjust suffer eternal incarceration and punishment:

Those who as long as life remained
Held brothers hateful, beat their parents, cheated
Poor men dependent on them; also those
Who hugged their newfound riches to themselves
And put nothing aside for relatives—
A great crowd this—then men killed for adultery,
Men who took arms in war against the right,
Not scrupling to betray their lords.[12]

The list of wrong-doers goes on, a great crowd of miscreants who broke the bonds of *pietas* during their earthly lives and suffer the consequences forever.

Virgil only discloses what sorts of sinner are condemned within the walls of Tartarus. Aeneas never actually sees them in midst of their eternal punishment because, as the Sibyl tells him, "no pure soul may cross the sill of evil" (*Aen.* 6.563). Dante decided not to do likewise; he acknowledges no such prohibition against entry into the "lost city" because the pilgrim must explore every inch of hell so that the reader can see it too—can take a close look at the lineup of highly individualized transgressors who sold out their city or lord, who foisted a tyrant on the people, "set up laws/ Or nullified them for a price" (*Aen.* 6. 621–622). Virgil decries categories of sinners from afar; the author of the *Comedy*, on the other hand, names names, gets up close and personal. Most importantly, and unlike Aeneas, the pilgrim sees himself in the damned.

Apart from what Dante learned about hell from earlier accounts or from the church iconography that was everywhere present (like the vivid Last Judgment mosaic in the Florentine baptistery, with its bestial, cannibalistic Satan), he also extrapolated from his own first-hand terrestrial observation. He got much of his material simply by looking around him. The *Inferno* is largely constructed of references to the wrongdoings of the Italian town Dante knew from birth or from those he lived in throughout his exilic wanderings. From the vantage of his own vulnerability—moving from place to place, earning his keep from nobility he likely held in little esteem—he gathered the scandals and notorious sinners of his age, the legendary inhumanities, the infighting of city-states perpetually at one another's throats, not to mention the evils of a church hierarchy he judged to be bent on turning the bride of Christ into a prostitute. His *Inferno*, in other words, is a withering portrait of our world if it were to be left to its worst devices. In it we see our lust for power when unalleviated by mercy, when the self is sovereign, frozen in obsessive monomania—always alone no matter how dense the crowd.

In canto 10, for instance, we encounter two shades, Farinata and Cavalcanti, who in life were united by ties that would seem strong enough to link them forever: Florentine citizenship, a common upper class, the same religion, and a betrothal of a son and a daughter. In hell they occupy a single sarcophagus and yet have no contact with one another, never acknowledge that their partner in close quarters even exists. Why? The men with everything in common belonged to different political factions—they represented two warring sides of the same Florentine coin. This turns out to be enough to make their division eternal. Dante speaks with each individually but never together. Despite the fact of their shared incarceration in the tomb they will forever call home, they have "nothing" in common.

In the course of his journey through hell the pilgrim descends gradually into what turns out to be a succession of concentric cityscapes that evoke ancient Babel, Troy, and Thebes as well as the city-states of central and northern Italy which Dante knew for himself. In canto after canto we move through gates and within walls, over bridges and around cemeteries, all of which remind him of this or that place on earth. Sometimes Dante encounters figures he recognizes from history and literature, but more often he keeps company with near contemporaries, even with people he knows personally. He is aghast to discover souls in hell he never expected to find there (the reverse will be true in purgatory). Some of them he treats with an affection and civility strangely out of place in the "dolorous kingdom."

Why make the damned appealing, even winsome? Dante may well have wanted (like Milton after him) to "justify the ways of God to men," but he made his task in this regard very difficult. Villains and monsters pose little problem, at least if one entertains a notion of an eternal hell as just desserts for wrong-doing. But what about the poignant lovebird Francesca, the public-spirited Farinata and doting father Cavalcanti, the courtly Pier della Vigne, the paternal Brunetto Latini, the eloquent Ulysses? And what of those who, like Virgil himself, are said to have erred only in lacking baptism? It is impossible to dismiss these vivid, multi-dimensional characters merely as instances of vice or sin personified.

Nor does Dante's pilgrim do so. He swoons after listening to Francesca's romance, praises his old teacher Brunetto to the skies, and is so intent upon hearing the words of the golden-tongued Ulysses that he nearly falls into the ditch of the false counselors. It is largely the force of context—this is hell, after all—and the warnings of Virgil to pay attention, that raise suspicions about the innocence of these characters and God's alleged injustice in damning them. Context matters as well as close attention to the beguiling words they speak, "innocent" as they are of the truth about themselves.

How the damned come to their eternal ends is shown to be a self-selection: the *Comedy* is based on the assumption that each individual chooses his or her place in the afterlife. Such a choice is the most important one anyone can make. It goes into effect only after one's last breath; until that moment, freedom of choice remains. After the end point, however, the decision is irrevocable. Dante is so fervent a believer in free will that he presents the damned as actually desiring their ends. Indeed, they rush toward Minos, the judge of hell, who discerns their deepest longing and sends them to their particular "reward." They are given for eternity what they most loved on earth. Their punishment is a version of their *modus vivendi*.

The justice of this assignment is called *il contrapasso*, or "the counter-penalty." The notion of sin being its own punishment prevails throughout *Inferno*, although it is only given a name in canto 28, and then by one of the damned in the circle of the Sowers of Discord. As a result of separating a father from a son, a king from his heir apparent, and therefore a kingdom from itself, Bertran de Born spends eternity with his head severed from his trunk. His damnation exemplifies his sin. Retrospectively, we discern the same logic of *contrapasso* at work in the eternal storm of the lustful or the boiling pitch of those who in life were mired in crooked deal-making. The crime becomes the punishment.

The contemporary reader, or perhaps a medieval person with a mind of his or her own, may resist some if not all of the poet's judgments. The *Divine Comedy* may "only" be a poem, an earnest fiction, but there is no gainsaying that Dante presumes to speak for God, as those with a high sense of calling so often do. The notions of sin which he devised for the structured cityscapes of hell—those of the appetite, violence, fraud, and treachery—are an odd amalgam of Aristotle, Cicero, and Catholic theology. The latter adds categories unimaginable to the ancient pagans whom the poet reveres and indeed relies on. (He would be nowhere without

Aristotle's *Nichomachean Ethics*, for instance.) Dante puts people of great worth and cultural cachet in the first circle of hell, in a pleasant Elysium where they nonetheless live in muted sadness, in desire but without hope. We learn that such worthies as Homer and Plato, not to mention beloved Virgil himself, are damned not for any wrong-doing but solely for lack of baptism—a specifically Christian requirement they could never meet, pertaining to a religious world they could never have known.

Difficulties with Dante's hell by no means end with its first circle, Limbo, which holds both unbaptized infants (traditionally meant to be there) and illustrious heroes from the pagan world (whose theologically unwarranted presence in Limbo caused an outcry from contemporary religious authorities). There are also subsequent "crimes" against divine justice that, from the perspective of many today, either seem like nothing of the sort, or about which the jury is out. Are pundits of the future, the sullen, suicides, homosexuals, the assassins of Caesar really so execrable?

For instance, we find usurers on the burning sands of the circles of the violent. Each burdened with the logo of his Italian banking family—all Florentines save for a single citizen of Padua—they suffer for having made money from money, for profiting from interest on a loan. The medieval church's condemnation here was not merely against taking exorbitant interest but of gaining interest at all. To support its view there were verses in Scripture, bits of Roman law, and Aristotle, who asserted that charging interest on a monetary loan was contrary to nature. Today, of course, ecclesiastical bodies of all sorts have their investments and depend for their ministry on investment return. From the time of the early-seventeenth century even the Vatican has had a bank, albeit with money-making designated for charitable purposes alone. It has also had its share of banking scandals over the course of time, as recently as the 1980s. The end of this uproar, as is often the case in the banking "community," was consolidation. After merger upon merger with other financial institutions, what was once the "Bank of the Holy Spirit" is now known simply (but certainly not without irony) as *Capitalia*. What once was sin is now good stewardship.

Dante descends into hell along a proverbially slippery slope where bad steadily leads to worst. Sins of the appetite are encountered first, and through them the corruption of the flesh, gathered into what we might think of as the outlying suburbs of the damned. Once inside the City of Dis, Dante experiences the corruption of a higher human faculty, the will, as it turns in various ways toward violence (against God, against others, against one's own self). Another descent takes the pilgrim down to Malebolge, a city within a city, where fraud provides examples of intelligence and ingenuity—*ingegno* or genius—that have been brought into the service of evil. Finally, Dante is lowered to the "bottom of the entire universe" (*Inf.* 32.8), where he finds the many permutations of treachery that erode human connection, whether to kin, those joined by covenant, guests, or a superior—in Satan's case, God. This realm of Cocytus is the *Comedy*'s concentration camp of purest evil, which the poet depicts as a realm not of fire, but of ice.

Cocytus is "the center/ to which all weight is drawn" (*Inf.* 32.73–74). Among the many things lost at this depth is the notion of *e pluribus unum*, one out of many. For a few almost unbearable cantos we witness the relentless desire of the radically private ego and the absolute refusal of partnership. The "high point" of Dante's most disturbing exposure of evil takes place in the company of traitors who broke faith with their political party. In this case, we have a count and an archbishop who represent corruption within the state as well as the church. Before we learn any of these particularities, however, we see an enactment of the hatred that is now their

only connection. These two men are posed in a grotesque rendering
of a back-to-front embrace—the "spoon" position of lovers. Instead
of embracing or sleeping, however, one man gnaws at the skull of
his partner:

> I saw two shades frozen in one hole
> so that one's head served as the other's cap;
> And just as he who's hungry chews his bread,
> one sinner dug his teeth into the other
> right at the place where brain is joined to nape . . .
>
> (32.125–129)

The precision of his description is elaborately gruesome, with the
two skulls so close that "one's head served as the other's cap"; the
placement of teeth on bone is "right at the place where brain is
joined to nape." Several readings are necessary to get beyond the
gore, to see, for instance, that Dante is making a parody of the
notion of unity. Two figures are frozen in one hole; one man's head
is the other's hat; one man's teeth are fused with another man's
skull. This vision of dog-eat-dog is also a perverse parody of the
Christian eucharist, with flesh becoming bread: this is *your* body
given for *me*. Hatred runs so deep here that only insensate cannibalism can suggest its fury.

Dante promises the avenger to share what he learns with the
living—if, that is, his tongue does not dry up on the spot. With
the possibility of a story perhaps too horrendous to tell, the next
canto opens with yet another visual assault: "That sinner raised
his mouth from his fierce meal,/ then used the head that he had
ripped open/ in back: he wiped his lips upon its hair" (33.1–3).
Then he speaks. The historical event Count Ugolino describes
took place in 1288 when Dante was 23, not in Florence but in

the neighboring city of Pisa. Its details are complex: two political animals, a count and an archbishop, forge alliances and make betrayals on all counts. In the end the archbishop wins the terrible game. He imprisons Ugolino and his four sons in a Pisan tower that, as a result of this incident, is known as the *Torre della Fame*, the "Tower of Hunger." For the fourteenth-century chronicler Giovanni Villani the sorry tale could be summarily dismissed as an instance of one traitor being betrayed by another.

That is what the facts look like from the outside. Dante, however, takes us where the historian cannot go except by poetic invention. He imagines what Ugolino thought and felt when no one else was there, at the very moment when the tower's door, normally opened at meal time to deliver the daily rations, was nailed shut. Both father and sons were dumbfounded by fear and disbelief: could this really be happening? But whereas Ugolino finds himself paralyzed—"I did not weep; within, I turned to stone"—his sons turn to him one by one, trying either to understand his pain or take it away. Day by day, one by one, they fall away, until Gaddo, the last to survive, throws himself at his father's feet and implores, "Father, why do you not help me?"

> And there he died; and just as you see me,
> I saw the other three fall one by one
> Between the fifth day and the sixth; at which,
>   now blind, I started groping over each;
> and after they were dead, I called them for
> two days; then fasting had more force than grief."
> When he had spoken this, with eyes awry,
> again he gripped the sad skull in his teeth,
> which, like a dog's, were strong down to the bone.
>   (33. 43–78)

With these last lines the poet forces us to realize the barely imagin-able: Ugolino's entire speech has taken place between mouthfuls. He begins by lifting his mouth to wipe it clean on the hairs of the head "he had ripped open/ in back" (33.3); he ends with a furious return to his "savage meal." Vengeance only momentarily takes the form of words, and then falls back into the inarticulate gnawing of teeth on bone.

This is what blind hatred looks like, and indeed there is in this horrible account abundant cause for hatred and revenge. A betrayed man and his four sons are starved to death; helpless, the father is forced to witness their suffering, which only quadruples his own. Ugolino confesses what this experience did to him: how he turned to stone, was unable to speak, bit his own flesh in a sign of frustration over his impotence and in rage at Ruggieri, the for-mer colleague in crime who engineered this evil. At the end of his speech he tells us that he groped over the corpses of his sons until "fasting had more power than grief." Either he too drops from starvation or he is driven by desperation to eat the flesh of his children. The text allows for both interpretations.

Is the Tower of Hunger a foreshadowing of other gruesome hells-on-earth we have come to know over the last hundred years: the Auschwitz and Bergen-Belsen camps, the killing fields of Cambodia, Rwanda, the Russian elementary school gymnasium at Beslan, Darfur? In all of these cases the membrane that separates our world from some kind of hell seems terrifyingly porous, gossa-mer, and the difference between Dante's Pisa and Satan's kingdom difficult to discern.

What is more, in the scene that Ugolino describes—as in the horrors of our own time—there is no *deus ex machina* to end the nightmare: no divine intervention, no ram in the thicket to sub-stitute for the human sacrifice, no rescue from the lion's den, no exit. "O hard earth, why did you not open up?" asks the distraught father as his children drop around him; so, too, might anyone else in his position. The suffering of children brings out the atheist in all of us, as Dostoevsky shows so brilliantly in *The Brothers Karamazov* through the outrage of the character Ivan. The torture and abuse of the innocent cry out to heaven for some kind of response. Yet none is forthcoming, and all attempts to explain or justify finally come to naught. If ever there were the occasion on which one might resolve, with Ivan, to "return the ticket to God"—say no thanks to any notion of a benevolent deity or providential order— the Tower of Hunger would seem to be it.

Or is it? For Ugolino, already blind, there is nothing other than darkness. Without a thought for the God who is apparently not there, he takes his dying hatred for Ruggieri into eternity and continues to gnaw on it forever. And yet, his narrative suggests (to us if not to him) that there was actually more than darkness at play in that tower. The place was not, after all, pitch black: it was not hell. There was "a little light" coming in through one small aperture. Although what is emphasized is the *tiny* size of this opening, the *brief* glimpses of sun and moonlight, we are told that light was there nonetheless.

Then there is another kind of illumination that Ugolino cannot recognize: the uncanny echo of Christ's Passion that his sons provide for him when unwittingly they bring Good Friday into the Tower of Hunger. It is as if he had four representations of Christ gathered around him, and through them recollections of Gethsemane and Golgotha: the sense of abandonment, the nails driven, the curtain rent, and the cry of "Father!" resounding three times in quick succession (vv. 51, 61, 69). Unlike Ugolino who turns in upon himself and cannot speak a single word to his boys, Anselmuccio (the diminutive of the name "Anselmo" is almost unbearable here) turns to him in genuine concern: "Father, you look so . . . What is wrong with you?" Seeing him bite both of his hands in rage, and mistaking his motivation as hunger, the boys offer *themselves* as bread, "Father, it will be much less pain for us if you eat of us." In doing so they unwittingly recall the night when Christ himself was betrayed and the words he spoke at table, "This is my body given for you." Finally, Gaddo throws himself at Ugolino's feet and cries out to him something very like *Eli, eli, lama sabbachtani*: "Father, why do you not help me?"[13]

Ugolino can make nothing of this gospel resonance, which, had he been able to acknowledge it, might have enabled him to discover the redemption offered in the Cross in the horror of his own situation, even in his children's suffering. He might have perceived the sign of the incarnate God's participation in the very depth of the human condition—and therefore had a cause of hope if not of rescue. But because he is deaf as well as blind to any divine presence in the Tower of Hunger, he is also cut off from those other last words of Christ which, had he been able to appropriate them, might have transformed his mortal ending and therefore his eternal life: "Father, forgive them, for they do not know what they are doing" (Luke 23:34); "Truly I tell you, today you will be with me in Paradise" (23:43); "Father, into your hands I commend my spirit" (23:46). Instead of this turning of himself over to God, he expires in hatred for Ruggieri. A starving man, his hunger is finally for revenge alone.

Revenge is precisely what Ugolino "gets" in the afterlife. Yet, as we can plainly see, it brings him no satisfaction. There is no end to it, no point at which the wasted skull of the archbishop will ever be consumed. It is all for nothing. Set over against this craving for vengeance—though never was grace less cheaply offered—Dante gives us the Christ story, the little ray of light in the darkness, the bread of heaven rather than the savage meal. Either cling to that sacrifice, the episode suggests, or construct a tower whose door will be nailed shut again and again on fresh victims.

All of this I believe to represent Dante's deep-felt theological conviction. It is also true, however, that when Ugolino finishes his speech and returns to the ravaged skull of Ruggieri we segue immediately to the words of the poet. Speaking in his authorial voice — the voice of the authority, which we have followed from the opening of the poem — he sounds more like the depraved Ugolino inveighing against his enemy than he does like Christ on Calvary:

> Ah, Pisa, you the scandal of the peoples
> of that fair land where *sì* is heard, because
> your neighbors are so slow to punish you,
>   may, then, Caprara and Gorgona move
> and build a hedge across the Arno's mouth,
> so that it may drown every soul in you!
>   For if Count Ugolino was reputed
> to have betrayed your fortresses, there was
> no need to have his sons brought to such a cross
>
> (33.79–87)

Whereas the pilgrim had no reaction to Ugolino's words, the poet gives himself away. His concern is finally not with Ugolino at all, either his past treachery or his pleas for vengeance; rather, it is with the innocent suffering of the man's children, who, through no fault of their own, were dragged into this horror on account of their father. In an immediate sense, of course, it was Archbishop Ruggieri who brought them to such a cross of suffering. Yet is not Ugolino also implicated in their deaths, accountable for his part in the construction of a political world in which betrayal and revenge are finally no respecter of persons? Did he not in effect help to build the Tower of Hunger that ended up devouring him and his children?

Dante seems to make this point by concluding his diatribe not with reference to Ruggieri or Ugolino but to the city the two traitors shared. Dante denounces their Pisa as the shame of Italy, a canker. Since the nearby towns are slow to move against their hateful neighbor, the poet takes it upon himself to invoke a catastrophe, to call for a lethal deluge to wipe the place clean by wiping it out altogether. Let two small offshore islands suddenly block the river Arno and so flood the city "that it may drown every person in you!" It was God who called for a flood at the beginning of human history because the earth "was corrupt in God's sight" (Gen 6:11). Later on, it was a man, Abraham, who interceded on the behalf of Sodom and Gomorrah by convincing the Lord not to destroy the city if ten just men could be found. Dante, however, is not interested in mercy's half measures. He usurps the divine perspective (and the prerogative that goes with it), proposing to avenge the deaths of the Pisan *innocenti* by drowning an entire civic population, one that no doubt would include its fair share of blameless children like "Anselmuccio."

On the one hand, Dante uses the Ugolino story to urge an end to violence and revenge. May no one ever again lose his children in a Tower of Hunger. Let no more little ones be dashed against the rocks. On the other hand, the poet calls for a vendetta on Pisa. Let Caprara and Gorgona dam up the river Arno—and let the "damnation" of Pisa begin.

Dante may be venting here, Italian style, with hyperbolic exuberance. Or he may be carefully staging this moment in order to show, through his own persona as poet, how difficult it is to withstand the impulse toward evil, especially for those who are in the business of righteousness. Or perhaps we are simply catching him with his guard down—seeing him as an angry man embittered by his experience of the political process, someone who writes this lengthy poem about divine judgment in order to settle accounts precisely, as he (and, of course, God) sees them. Maybe this is what happens when you descend to the bottom of the universe in your terrible mind's eye and then describe it so lucidly. You take on the attributes of that angel of light who, even before Adam and Eve, wanted to be divine. You destroy one group of innocents in order to avenge another. It may be as perilous to be a connoisseur of evil as it is to pretend that it does not exist.

Is there anything redeemable about hell—the ground floor of the medieval three-story universe, the tick-tock of Father Arnall's "ever, never," the cultivation of terror for the purposes of love? The creeds we recite in church speak of Christ's descent into hell (not an event recorded in Scripture) and of "the life of the world to come" (something of a blank check); but those who formulated these core confessions of the faith left the matter pretty much at that. I am inclined to do so as well, fully aware that the tradition itself has gone much further. There may be as many Christians who firmly believe in a place of eternal retribution as there are those like me who find it abhorrent. They have Christian history (and Dante!) on their side; I have questions. To what possible end would God punish a creature forever—would it be the maintenance of divine purity, the unimpeded exercise of wrath, the right of total refusal? Why?

Those unable to "sign on" to hell but unable to let it go can take refuge in interpretation. Origen famously believed that not even Satan in the end could withstand a divine love that would be "all in all" no matter what. Henry Ward Beecher turned to psychology. He tried to persuade his congregation to go beyond the "foolish constructions" of his own father's religion and understand that hell was a "state of consciousness" entirely within their control. Give yourself over to "hell thoughts" ("such as envy, malice, hatred, or sin in any form") and you consign yourself to hell. Such is the power of negative thinking. Conversely, put yourself in a heavenly state of mind and the Kingdom of Heaven is within you, today, "in the routine of life."[14] On the whole issue of eternity it would be kind to say that Beecher simply made a side-step. The life of the world to come mattered a great deal less than right now.

Vacuous liberalism? Perhaps. Yet no one would bring such a charge against Pope John Paul II, who in the summer of 1999 felt impelled to offer the faithful an understanding of the afterlife that would be more intelligible or—dare one say this of a conservative pope?—more acceptable to contemporary people. Although turning to the subject of the afterlife still several years before his death in 2005, he may have felt the need at the time not only to meet the perceived needs of his flock but to clarify for himself what the world to come might be. What exactly was he facing in his own illness and advanced age?

Like Beecher with his reformulation of damnation as a "state of consciousness," but with infinitely more *gravitas*, John Paul understood traditional teaching in the light of human interiority, along with the help of the existentialist philosophy he studied in his youth. Respectful of all that had gone before, he did not go so far as to speak of "foolish constructions." Nonetheless, he wanted to free Catholics from too literal a reading of Scripture as well as the more lurid aspects of the tradition. He would be taken to task for this by Catholic traditionalists as well as a viper's tangle of Protestant bloggers and Internet Kilroys who, in books, videos, and CDs, all swore to have been to an infernal *somewhere*, not merely in a state of mind.

According to Pope John Paul, hell lasts forever and is the result of human choice: no one is forced into damnation. But it is also not a place in the sense of a material location. In other words, what Dante saw and what Michelangelo painted—"hateful fiends . . . gnawing at the skulls of suffering sinners"—is the equivalent of pious tradition; it is not dogma. Hell should not be thought of as underground or as extending any "where" else. Rather, it is a spiritual condition, a "state of complete frustration and emptiness of life without God . . . the state of those who freely and definitively separate themselves from God."[15] It is not necessary to literalize hell or turn "frustration and emptiness" into geography. It is enough to imagine what it means, to sense the interior abyss that Gerard Manley Hopkins described in one of his so-called "terrible sonnets": "O the mind, mind has mountains; cliffs of fall / Frightful, sheer, no-man-fathomed. Hold them cheap / May who ne'er hung there."[16] Once the "cliffs of fall" are confronted, only a madman would not pull back from their edge.

This pulling back from the edge is one way to understand repentance, a turning around from one reality to face another. It may be that such a change in orientation does not take place unless, in the language of Alcoholics Anonymous, there is a "bottoming out." Perhaps this is the purpose of thinking about hell: to bottom out, to recognize the black hole that each of us (or all of us together) might become, to imagine the Towers of Hunger we could construct for ourselves or for one another.

One need not have a mind for eternity in order to take such prospects seriously. Nor does the hell within us need to be so grandiose. There is the slip and slide of evil, the coldness of heart that might well become the frozen waste Dante imagines around Satan. More common, however, is the sudden chill of ordinary days—little cruelties of pride or envy that, bit by bit, accumulate, and gradually bring us closer to nothingness.

For me, Christian tradition has no need for new Gehennas. There is enough infernal weeping and gnashing of teeth on record to last for eternity. But perhaps there is some good that can come of considering what it would actually be like if our capacity to know and love God were to atrophy or die away entirely. What would happen if we succeeded in living for ourselves alone, or if revenge went unchecked? To become conscious of what John Paul II called a "state of complete frustration and emptiness of life" may be the first step in moving away from it. Isn't it time to say, "Look at what's happening to us; we must change our lives"?

Back in the early-fourteenth century Dante thought it was. For better and for worse he continues to force his readers to stare into the abyss, to acknowledge that everyone is capable of horrendous acts—and to acknowledge that they are happening right now. In the larger trajectory of his poem, however, the poet also does a great deal more than this. For his vision of evil does not have the last word: the *Inferno* opens the door first on the *Purgatorio* and then on its complete obverse, the *Paradiso*. After a season in hell the poet moves us through the experience of human transformation—how one's life *can* be changed—and into an approximation of beatitude. He insists on the big picture. And rightly so, for what is essential to any healthy examination of evil, lest a focus on negation get the better of us, is a compelling sense of the good from which evil deviates. To this end, a sober look at darkness can make you hunger and thirst for light, help you realize that you are actually *starving* for it. This growth in appetite is precisely what we see when Dante takes on the second leg of his journey through the "undiscovered country"—to purgatory.

Contented
in the Fire

PURGATORY

The two poles of the eternal afterlife, hell and heaven, are common property for all Christians. Whether we believe in them or not, they are quite simply there, part of our inheritance and cropping up in high and low culture alike. Purgatory is something else—time-bound, temporary, specifically Roman Catholic, and relatively late in its arrival on the otherworld scene.

My own encounter with it took place when I was a teenager in the late 1950s, in the days before Vatican II and therefore at the tail end of its glory days. Happily, it also came to me wholly apart from the theological wrangling that had long embittered dealings between Catholics, who believed in it ardently, and Protestants, who thought it was hogwash. Because my Protestant-Catholic extended family tacitly agreed never to discuss religion, silence kept the peace among us. If anyone believed in purgatory it went without saying. But my eyes and ears were open. One day, on my own in Manhattan and always a sucker for church-going, I followed a Fifth Avenue-throng into St. Patrick's Cathedral and took in the twelve side altars that flanked the nave. Each one was focused on some object of devotion: a moment in the life of the

Savior or of the Virgin Mary, particular saints with a local following, Veronica's veil, his and her sacred hearts. Fascinated by
the whole scene, I began to keep track of the little placards that
also appeared at every shrine. In exchange for the recitation of a
certain prayer, one could get a given number of purgatorial days
"off" for the soul the petitioner had in mind, that is, for someone
deceased, who was now among the faithful departed.

Thanks to second-hand acquaintance with the late nineteenth-
century Baltimore Catechism, which was required reading for
so many of my friends, I understood the basic concepts at work.
Anyone who dies in a state of grace—that is, baptized and with
even a last-breath appeal to God for forgiveness—was on the way
to salvation. There should be no anxiety on that score. He or she
was most probably not yet ready, however, to enter the divine
presence. Except for those very few whose entire lives had been
an extended practice of contrition—the overwhelmingly saintly—
most people would die owing a debt for sins that had not suffi-
ciently been repented. Divine justice demanded satisfaction; so too
did divine perfection. Since an encounter with God required absolute purity, the rank-and-file soul would need to be cleansed of a
lifetime's accretion of sin before the promised face-to-face vision
with the Trinity could be enjoyed. They would not be ready to
"see straight." There was work to be done, and purgatory was the
place to do it.

This made sense, although the ecclesiastical language was
strange to my ears and the sheer confidence of the Baltimore
Catechism breathtaking. How could anyone know these things
with such clarity and assurance? I was drawn in, however,
because purgatory seemed to answer a need. By my teens I had
found the notion of an eternal hell unworthy of God and impossible to believe in. Heaven, although an article of faith I was happy

to affirm, was a luminous "cloud of not-knowing." Purgatory, by contrast, seemed as if it should be invented if it didn't exist already. Although the expression "No pain, no gain" was not in currency at the time, its sentiment summed up what I thought purgatory had to offer—suffering for a purpose, not as an end unto itself. Furthermore, the souls of the faithful departed could grow gradually beyond their lifetime's limitations. They could make progress, which is a concept dear to the American heart. Best of all, purgatory offered an opportunity for us, the living, to perform works of love for those we keep on loving long after their deaths.

Suddenly the idea of the communion of saints became vivid, and with it the possibility that we could help those who had died even as we were told to assist them when they were very much alive—by praying for them. Unlike the Reformers, I liked the open door between this world and the next. Mourners needn't be limited to keening, or keeping a stiff upper lip, or telling poignant or embarrassing stories about the deceased. We could name them before God; we could remember them at the Eucharist along with "angels and archangels and all the company of heaven."

Nonetheless, I had a hard time with the thought that grace could be managed in as efficient a way as the side altar prayer-exchange suggested. I was also troubled by the idea that there were days in the afterlife that sped by in response to prayers recited. The mechanics of quid pro quo were disturbing. Therefore, no matter how provocative my walkabout in St. Patrick's may have been, I ultimately put the whole business behind me when I left the cathedral. Purgatory—like white First Communion outfits, meatless Fridays, and weeping statues—was meant for Roman Catholics, not for me.

Where did this uniquely Catholic space in the afterlife come from? According to Jacques LeGoff, its most renowned contemporary historian, purgatory's "birth certificate" was an official letter written by Innocent IV in 1254, in which the pope defined as an actual place what had long been thought of as a vaguely conceived process.[17] Exactly twenty years later, that definition was consolidated at the Second Council of Lyons. Those who died after receiving penance, but without having time to complete it fully, could do so after death in the "temporary fire" of purgatory. The church declared that this was all "according to the traditions and authority of the Holy Fathers," as Innocent put it. But this claim was something of a stretch, even if the faithful had been praying for the dead from early on. Such figures as Tertullian and Augustine wrote evocatively about purgative "fires" and "pains," but always short of affirming a distinct location. By the end of the twelfth century, however, theologians began to speak specifically of a *purgatorium* where a soul's rehabilitation took place in the midst of "real" material fire and for a specific period of time.

The Catholic Church did not specify officially where purgatory actually was or elaborate on the mechanics of purgatorial pain. So too in our own time. In his 1999 papal audiences on the afterlife, John Paul II counseled the faithful not to fixate on any specific location or be swept away by the wild fancies of popular piety; purgatory indicated not place or a location, but something integral to the human condition. It should be enough to speak of "purificatory penalties" and to focus on what the living might do to assist the dead. To this end the Second Council of Lyons enumerated "suffrages" that were no doubt already in operation among the people then and that continued to animate St. Patrick's Cathedral until fifty years ago: "the sacrifice of the mass, prayers, alms, and other works of piety that the faithful customarily offer on behalf of others of the faithful according to the institutions of the Church."[18] One was not to dwell on purgatory itself but rather concentrate on

how to aid those who were making their way through it—where-
or what-ever it was.

Scholars dispute why purgatory "happened" when it did. They
offer a wide variety of social, economic, and legal factors as well
as no less complex developments within the "mind of the church,"
such as an upsurge in interest in penance and its procedures. The
great medieval theologians were happy by and large to stay with
the significance of purgation and let the fact of pain suffice. Thomas
Aquinas, for instance, admits that there are many things alleged by
"pious tradition" or "common law" which the faithful should entertain only with a grain of salt. They should also realize that there
are limits to this speculation since we have neither clear guidelines
from Scripture nor convincing arguments on this question from
anywhere else. On the other hand, Aquinas was willing to concede
this much: the suffering of those being "saved by fire" is beyond
anything known or even imagined in the flesh. Though temporary,
it would be terrible. Worse, however, would be the awful sense of
separation from God—a loss barely perceived by most "faithful"
souls in their mortal lives but intolerable in the hereafter.[19]

In contrast to the theologians, the popular preachers of fear
outdid themselves with hair-raising descriptions of what went
on in purgatory. So, too, did the afterlife visionaries who wrote
in the centuries before Dante, both in Latin and the vernacular. An arsenal of horror was deployed in these accounts: pits of
fire, mountains of ice, furnaces and ovens, punishing angels and
devouring beasts. Although purgatory's whereabouts was subject
to dispute—it turns out that the popular imagination demanded
something less abstract than a "state of existence"—it was most
often assumed to be subterranean and ghastly, an antechamber to
hell or even a portion of its upper reaches. In short, it was like hell,
but only for a time.

There are anticipations of purgatory in medieval narratives such as *The Vision of Drythelm, Tundale's Vision*, and *St. Patrick's Purgatory*. But not until the thirteenth-century's *Vision of Thurkill* do we find a representation of a purgatory independent of hell and functioning as an autonomous (temporal) realm alongside the eternal realms of damnation and salvation. This autonomy is not immediately apparent. When the visionary Thurkill first sees the *purgatorium*—the word appears in the text—it can easily be mistaken for the place of eternal punishment. Many infernal features are on hand: lakes of scalding fire alternating with plunge pools of cold salty water, and an arching bridge over which souls make their tortuous way. Thurkill sees the souls groveling, trying to cross over the bridge barefoot. They are alternately pierced through by the sharp stakes they grab hold of to keep from falling over and by thorns that crop up underfoot on every side. He watches as they roll on their lacerated bellies, "dreadfully bloody and pierced all over," as if they were among the damned seen below. Yet they are not. Unlike those condemned to suffer eternally, they are only in agony for a season. Nor is their purgatorial pain merely torture: it has a purpose as well as an end, as the souls discover when they complete their terrible crossing-over and find themselves at last in a place of rest and refreshment.

Just as their suffering is only for the time being, so too is purgatory itself. It will end precisely when Christ returns in glory to judge the quick and the dead. At this point heaven and hell will take exclusive hold on the afterlife and the middle space of transformation, like time itself, be no more. Until the final trumpet sounds, however, the souls work out their salvation with fear and trembling, making their way through a realm so horrible that the ghost of Hamlet's father cannot bring himself to describe it:

I am thy father's spirit;
Doom'd for a certain term to walk the night,
And for the day confin'd to waste in fires,
Till the foul crimes done in my days of nature
Are burnt and purg'd away. But that I am forbid
To tell the secrets of my prison-house,
I could a tale unfold whose lightest word
Would harrow up thy soul; freeze thy young blood;
Make thy two eyes, like stars, start from their spheres;
Thy knotted and combined locks to part,
And each particular hair to stand on end
Like quills upon the fretful porcupine:
But this eternal blazon must not be
to ears of flesh and blood.

(1.5.9–22)

Note that Hamlet Senior says next to nothing about his own daytime "waste in fires."[20] He speaks only of what would happen to *us*, flesh and blood, were he simply to speak his mind. Were we to receive his unrestrained report, our souls would freeze, our hair stand on end, our eyes burst from their sockets. He provokes our fear through his refusal to talk. Entirely missing from his account are the positive aspects of purgation that the vision literature adumbrates and that Dante develops most fully. We are given no sense of a soul's growing, of a restored person finally leaving the prison-house to take up a new life in glory. This may be because the good news of purgatory was often lost in the penitential admonition to take stock. Or perhaps we glimpse only the horror because at this point the ghost is but a newcomer to his ordeal. He is still making his way through the "prison-house" and unaware of his ultimate release. "Doom'd" is all he feels himself to be when in fact his doom, however long-lasting it may prove to be, is only "for a certain term." This too will pass.

Shakespeare penned this speech in what was an officially (if newly) Protestant sixteenth-century England, a reformed realm in which purgatory could be dismissed, according to the Church of England's *Articles of Religion*, as one of the pope's detestable enormities, "a fond thing, vainly invented, and grounded upon no warranty of Scripture, but repugnant to the Word of God." John Calvin was equally withering: purgatory, he wrote in *Institutes of the Christian Religion*, is a "deadly fiction of Satan which nullifies the cross of Christ, inflicts unbearable contempt upon God's mercy, and overturns and destroys our faith."

This is, of course, the fiery discourse of the Protestant Reformers, but a good century before these hard-line positions were taken purgatory had also proved an obstacle for the Eastern Orthodox. In 1453, for instance, the Greeks walked out of the Council of Florence—a vain stab at a reunion of East and West—when they found themselves at odds with their hosts over a number of issues, among them the state of the redeemed soul after death. While they allowed the efficacy of prayers for the faithful departed, and affirmed that there could be some form of afterlife purification, they rejected Rome's insistence on an actual intermediate place for punishments, on temporal fire as the agent of purity, and on the admissibility of making offerings for the dead. Prayers for the faithful departed, yes; temporal fire and indulgences (time-off from suffering obtained as the result of good deeds by the living), no.

Less than a century later, Protestant reaction was far more vehement. In the first place, purgatory was dismissed as a "fond invention" because it had no proper warrant in Scripture. Yes, there was a clutch of verses, the same ones that the Latin apologists had also brandished for their Eastern counterparts. Among these the most explicit and therefore the weightiest was 2 Maccabees 12:42–45, which speaks of making a good and salutary gift in the Temple as "atonement for the dead, so that they might be delivered from their sin." But because Maccabees was not to be found in the Protestant Old Testament (or the Jews' *Hebraica veritas*), it had no canonical authority. Likewise, the legitimate passages the Roman apologists habitually invoked — Matthew 12:32 (the sin against the Holy Spirit cannot be forgiven "either in this age or in the age to come") and 1 Corinthians 3:11–15 (a person's work will be "revealed by fire" either to suffer loss or to be saved) — had all been grossly misinterpreted, forced by papal "sophists" to mean something they clearly did not.

Protestants also viewed with great suspicion the way belief in purgatory, and the intercessory practices that grew up around it, made the separation of the living from the dead less than absolute. People could be lulled into thinking that they could put off until tomorrow — after death — the repentance they failed to do today. They also argued that purgatory diminished the unique work of the redeemer. According to John Calvin, because "the blood of Christ is the only satisfaction for the sins of believers, the sole purgation, what remains but to say that purgatory is simply a dreadful blasphemy against Christ?" And then, of course, there was the whole business of indulgences, the works-righteousness of pilgrimages and votive masses, the ease with which alms and "certificates" could devolve into bribes or payments — all of it flimflam from the Reformers' perspective.

This heated controversy was ancient history by the time I began my theological education in the late sixties. Purgatory never entered the picture during my three years at Union Seminary, nor has it ever arisen in any serious conversation with Roman Catholic friends. Imagine my surprise then, when I had a vision of

my deceased father in what I can only call purgatorial surround-
ings. I am sorry to report no lifting of the veil for twenty-three
minutes, let alone for ninety: at best I enjoyed a visionary split
second. Nonetheless, at the time, and now in retrospect, I believe
I had an insight into what purgatory might mean, or even, for all I
know, what it might be. What I discovered was neither a place nor
a "state of consciousness" but a scenario—or, better yet, a jerky
sequence of still images such as you see on surveillance camera
footage. I had a glimpse into *something*.

My father died in 1988, by which time I had moved my parents
from New York to West Hartford, Connecticut, and the extended
family dwindled to a handful of people with whom I'd lost touch.
Because two years had gone by since Dad's death, and no one else
had gotten around to organizing a proper funeral, I felt out of a
primitive sense of what the dead are owed that I needed to make a
move. I asked the parish priest at a local church if it would be possible to offer the next Saturday morning Eucharist in memory of
my father. I wasn't entirely sure what I was asking for. I only knew
it was time to get those ashes out of my study closet.

The priest was happy to oblige, and so, with the very odd
assortment of people who go to an Episcopal Eucharist on a
Saturday morning, I prayed for the repose of Thomas William
Hawkins, Sr. During the service my mind wandered, as it inevitably does in church. I soon found myself thinking about my father
with regret over things done and left undone. Ours had not been
a relationship made in heaven, for which I had come more and
more to blame myself. Nor had I ever reconciled myself to the
extraordinary caution that had characterized his entire life and
that had inhibited mine. Anything new was fearsome, everything
cost too much, and taking risks or living improvidently was what
other people did, not us.

Imagine my surprise, then, when at some point in the liturgy I suddenly beheld my father in what looked like a casino, gleefully wasting money with a zest I had never actually seen in him. A depressed survivor of the Great Depression, he had always been pathologically careful *not* to spend. Money was to be held on to, saved for a rainy day or simply saved. It was never wasted. But there he was in my mind's eye, in the fluorescent light of a gambling hall—quarters flying, one-armed bandits pumping away—as if there were no tomorrow. He was definitely not in repose; he was a very happily agitated man in full-smile mode. Who *was* this person? I wanted to know him.

When I came to my senses afterward, wisely making no mention of any of this to the priest at the door, I wondered if I had seen my father in purgatory as he was learning to let go and have fun, no longer burdened by the need to save but free at last to be crazy and irresponsible. At first, playing the slot machines would have been painful, perhaps even a torment, because wasting money was against his personal religion. It was the unforgivable sin. But maybe this is what happens when you die: the arms of mercy that receive you set you loose in a place where you would not otherwise be caught dead. Maybe they bid you do the opposite of what you'd done in life, nudge you to go to the other side of the territory you had mistakenly confused with reality. Rather than being as comfortable as an old shoe, as satisfying as a long-held dream come true, maybe the afterlife came as a rude shock. Maybe it hurt.

"Hurting" was largely what purgatory was supposed to be about. Thanks to what LeGoff called the church's move toward "infernalization," the idea of terrible punishment has prevailed for centuries. Even today, in churches throughout Latin America where purgatory continues to hold the grip that has otherwise been lost in the developed world, you can still find representations of souls almost totally submerged within painted flames, their agonized faces crying out for rescue. Dante certainly accepted this notion of purgatorial "hurting," along with the other theological premises sketched above, but he completely altered its atmosphere or "feel" by challenging the primacy traditionally given to suffering. His purgatorial spirits are, as Virgil explains even before the journey takes place, *contenti nel foco*, "content within the fire." The reason is, they have something wonderful to look forward to: "they hope to reach/—whenever that may be—the blessed people" (*Inf.*1.119–120). The poet was not the first to make hopefulness the hallmark of purgatory, nor would he be the last. Two hundred years after him Catherine of Genoa wrote a treatise on purgatory that speaks of its joys as ardently as she would of its pains.[21] But no one else has ever come near the totality of his rendering or the extent of his make-over.

Dante began with an overhaul of locale. Instead of imagining purgatory as an underground ante-chamber to hell, he placed it ranging along the terraced sides of an immensely high mountain that rose up from the otherwise empty seas of the Southern Hemisphere. It stood at the antipodes from Jerusalem, which was believed to be at the center of the inhabited world. The mountain was beautiful, adorned with art, and crowned by the lush fertility of a Garden of Eden that was watered by just two rivers, not the biblical four. There was Lethe, borrowed from the classical world, in which the rehabilitated souls forget past guilt; and there was Eunoe, Dante's invention, in whose waters the former penitents recall the moments of grace to which they were oblivious when alive.

What is perhaps most immediately striking about this above-ground reimagining is that Dante's purgatory is not shrouded in the traditional gloom but bathed in gorgeous light. The pilgrim arrives there just before dawn, when the planet Venus is said to make the whole sapphire-hued east "smile." From this first starry moment onward, his journey takes place (or bides its time) *en plein air*. His path is illumined during the day by a sun that rises and sets in great beauty. At night, when the sun is "silent," there is a brilliant recompense in luminous planets and constellations. Freed from the claustrophobia of hell, we find ourselves not only newly-risen from the grave but part of a cosmological pull toward the heavens that in every sense draws the penitents upward.

Also striking is the way Dante constructs his purgatory to be not hell's close cousin but its mirror opposite. He imagines it by contrast, as if in *Purgatorio*, the *Comedy*'s second canticle, he was programmatically developing the dark negative of the first. Whereas the pilgrim descends into hell, moving to the sinister left, he climbs the mountain always according to the right hand. In hell he moves from the sins of the flesh to those of the will and the intellect as he goes from bad to worst. Conversely, the purgatorial pilgrim starts out with the most grievous disorders in intellect and will before passing on to those of the flesh. While the gravitational pull of hell is strongest at the bottom, the pilgrim finds himself almost in flight as he approaches the mountain's summit. The contrasts continue. Rather than being like hell, therefore, Dante's purgatory is as systematically unlike it as possible. From a hole in the ground he gives us a mountain skyscraper; from a descent into darkness, a rising up into light.

The mountain is divided into three discrete sections. At the base are gathered souls not yet ready to begin the hard climb. There are those who repented only in the last desperate moment of their lives; those who, through sloth, barely repented at all; and those who were so preoccupied with worldly advancement that they neglected to prepare themselves for the life to come. The souls "ripen" as they develop the necessary spiritual strength to begin the serious business of rebirth. When they are ready to do so, they work their way up the terraced walkways, each dedicated to one of the seven deadly sins. Appearing in the order first established by Gregory the Great in the sixth century, these are first Pride, then Envy, Wrath, Sloth, Avarice-Prodigality, and Gluttony. Last, and truly least, comes Lust. The weightiest sins are located at the bottom of the structure, those of lesser "gravity" arranged at the top.

The terraces lie just inside a massive gateway, with an angel guardian and an elaborate entry rite that involves the inscription on the pilgrim's forehead of seven Ps. Each is a sign of the residue of a *peccatum*, a sin that penance will erase. Once within the Gate, repentance begins in earnest with painful self-confrontation and arduous acts of contrition. Yet as the poet counsels his readers on the first of the terraces, the point of the process is not pain but gain: "Don't dwell upon the form of punishment," he says, "consider what comes after that" (10.109–110).

What we are *not* meant to dwell on is a variety of penitential ordeals: the heavy burdens borne on the shoulders of the proud, the sewn-up eyes of the envious, the corridor of purifying fire through which the lustful make their way, who are equally divided between what we would now call heterosexuals and homosexuals. To see each penance enacted, moreover, is to foresee its eventual termination. The proud will cast off their dead weights, the blinded envious will see, the lustful will step out of the fire and into the Edenic garden that blooms verdant and welcoming on the other side of lust's "burning path" (26.28). Rather than being a penitentiary, in other words, purgatory is a hospital for the healing of brokenness. It is a school for the learning of truth, an incubator in which worms grow up to be butterflies, a conservatory where soloists become a chorus, and where speakers develop a use for "we" and "us" instead of only "I" and "me." Life sentences are not served here so much as lives are rewritten.

Other analogies, however anachronistic, also spring to mind. Purgatory is a naturalization center where refugees from earth — Florence and Pisa, or the places where any of us live now — learn how to become citizens of the City of God. Or to put it yet another way, the whole experience of the mountain can be likened to psychoanalysis, where the patient painfully unties the knots of the past so as to live more freely in an unencumbered future. Vice is a sickness to be cured, not merely a blemish to be burned away. Whereas hell was all about the compulsion to repeat, an endless replay of the sinner's "song of myself," purgatory by contrast is dynamic, dedicated to change and transformation. It concerns the rebirth of a self free at last to be interested in other souls and other things. It is all about renewal, about the experience of becoming new.

What the souls in purgatory have in common — no matter how ill-prepared they may have been at their time of death, no matter the extent to which they are still works in progress — is their final turn toward God. Self-involvement is essentially what Dante understands sin to be, a destructive narcissism whose impulse is to erase the other in order to secure one's own "divine right." Every compartment of hell is full of fresh examples. In the course of moving through it, moreover, we also see that solipsism is never a victimless crime, but is always social in its effect. A private kiss can bring down a kingdom, a single counterfeiter debase a currency.

The opposite is true as well. We learn in *Purgatorio* that virtue can open up locked doors, can bring a new understanding of life that amounts to a reinvention of the status quo. Provenzan Salvani, Tuscany's most arrogant grandee in Dante's day, set up shop as a beggar in the Campo of Siena, "to free his friend from suffering in Charles's prison,/ humbling himself, he trembled in each vein"

(11.136–38). What but love could have led such a person to "set aside all shame" and prize someone other than himself?

Love is the key to purgatory, as Virgil explains in canto 17, the *Comedy*'s midpoint. The terraces of the mountain are designed with the redress of disordered love in mind, vice paired with virtue as the penitent moves from the grip of the one to the freedom of the other. The most grievous sins are clustered lower down, where alienation from love is most apparent. (Arrogance is considered more deleterious than lust, for instance.) Those sins closer to the top represent a mistaken or excessive desire, which once led souls to pursue a lesser good with the zeal that should have been reserved for God. Food was misused, creature comforts made too much of, sex pursued in ways that were compulsive and unhealthy. The journey up the mountain, therefore, deals first with the disorders of the higher faculties before turning to those associated with the flesh.

On each of the terraces, a particular failure in love is suffered, rectified, and transformed into a virtue that corresponds to the vice. The proud, as I've noted, suffer the heavy burden of their egos, which are represented by the rock under which each one is bowed. Their punishment is to carry this increasingly oppressive and false persona until they can willingly let go of it. When they are able to do so, they stand tall—which is to say, stand humbly—at last free of what they mistakenly thought to be their true self. The imprisonment of the vice is transformed into the freedom of the virtue. The self-important worm becomes the angelic butterfly it was always meant to be.

Throughout this work of transformation the souls in effect "go to church": they worship themselves clean and sing themselves free. The Beatitudes are chanted on each terrace, as are other prayers, hymns, and psalms, such as the *Miserere*, the *Te lucis ante*, the *Salve regina*. But the Beatitudes have a particular role to play. They are recollections of Jesus' Sermon on *another* mount, indications of the virtues that have been acquired along the purgatorial way, and foretastes of life in the heavenly city that is the pilgrim's destination. They are also the antiphonal response to the erasure of each of the seven sins that were marked on the pilgrim's forehead when he began his ascent. A rhythm then takes over. On the Terrace of Pride, for instance, an angel sings, "Blessed are the poor in spirit" when the penitent makes an exit and the first *peccatum* is whisked away. One expects to hear the singing of the corollary, "for theirs is the kingdom of heaven," but does not. All such corollaries are left unvoiced on the mountain but are by no means forgotten: each is embodied in the person of the penitent who now enters into a new stage of beatitude. In every case the angel gives the versicle and the penitent *is* the response. The newly humble soul, "poor in spirit," is ready to inherit the kingdom.

How quickly this liberation takes place depends on the individual soul, the extent of past sins, and the assistance that has been given within the communion of saints. The church calculated time in purgatory as a sentence measured out in years and even days. You served your time and then were freed. Dante also avails himself of this concept on occasion. The ancient Roman poet Statius, for instance, tells us in *Purgatorio* 22 that he spent five centuries "working" on prodigality before tackling his sin of sloth for an additional four hundred years. Not sharing the faith with anyone turns out to have its consequences: as a closet Christian, a *chiuso cristian*, his lukewarmness left him on his own for hundreds of years, with no one living to assist him in his spiritual work.

Yet the overall spirit of the *Purgatorio* is not to emphasize the calculation of years-to-be-spent. We understand that the proud are released from their burdensome egos not so much in answer to an external clock as in response to their own maturation. They will "terminate," to recall the analogy of psychoanalysis, when their spiritual work, their conversion of virtue into vice, is complete. When that happy time comes, the Mountain shakes with joy as the other penitents sing out *Gloria in excelsis Deo*, as indeed they do for Statius when he "has done" with Sloth.

At the summit of this entire penitential structure stands the Garden of Eden, the "nest" into which humankind was born and wherein the purged souls celebrate their spiritual rebirth before moving on to the heavenly paradise. Dante's decision to plant Eden atop the mountain of purgatory was a master stroke of theological geography—one of his many bright and original ideas. By crowning penance with innocence, he illustrates that what was lost to humanity by the First Adam has been restored in the redemption wrought by the Second. (We owe this typology to Paul: "for as all die in Adam, so all will be made alive in Christ," 1 Cor 15:22). As if this weren't enough, the poet has positioned Eden at the antipodes from Jerusalem, the place where, according to the Apostles' Creed, Christ "suffered under Pontius Pilate, was crucified, dead, and buried. He descended into Hell. The third day he rose again from the dead." Dante gives us paradise regained, a territory that is "rooted and grounded" (Eph 3:17) in Christ.

Along with the theological reinvention of both the earthly globe and the afterlife's middle kingdom is the elaborate, emotionally charged encounter that unfolds in the Garden—the pilgrim's meeting with Beatrice. Here some background is in order. According to the *Vita nuova*—a spiritual autobiography written in poetry and prose at the beginning of Dante's career—Beatrice overwhelmed him from that moment in their childhood when he first set eyes on her. The ensuing story is stylized, filled with swoons, misunderstandings, and hopeless idealizations—adolescent, in short. Yet for all the highfalutin' romance, a core truth emerges. Through the eyes of love we see something more than we had ever bargained on. Dante encounters another person more real than himself, and a power that transforms everything: "I glowed with a flame of charity that moved me to forgive all who had ever injured me; and if at that moment someone had asked me a question, about anything, my only reply would have been: 'Love.'" After Beatrice's death, she returns to him in a series of dreams, and then in a vision of her in divine glory that is so beyond his present powers to describe that he has to defer writing about it until a later time: "Thus, if it shall please Him by whom all things live that my life continue for a few years, I hope to compose concerning her what has never been written in rhyme of any woman."[22]

Undertaken roughly fifteen years after the *Vita nuova* —with other works of philosophy and linguistics begun but left unfinished, as well as rough erotic poems addressed to other women — the *Comedy* becomes that occasion. It is Beatrice who activates the pilgrim's journey to God at the very beginning of the narrative, and it is the prospect of seeing her again that enables him to descend into hell and endure the pain of purgatory. Her name needs to work wonders, and does. To seduce the pilgrim to step into the cleansing flames of the terrace of Lust, Virgil coaxes him, "Now see, son: this/ wall stands between you and Beatrice" (*Purg.* 27.35–36). When Dante still holds back, his guide tells him the whitest of lies: "I seem to see her eyes already!" At last standing before him in Eden, Beatrice is veiled and therefore hidden from view. Nonetheless, she is still unmistakably herself, and so is he. Trembling now the way he used to when she was alive, he confesses, "I felt love's ancient power" (30.39), and "I know the signs of the ancient flame" (30.48). Veiled though she is, and surrounded by figures of the seven virtues, the encounter is undeniably hot.

We are no longer in the land of the Baltimore Catechism, or elsewhere in "normative" Christianity, for that matter. Nor do other renderings of purgatory, renowned for its flames, imagine anything even remotely like *this* kind of fire. Thus, once we enter Eden, the familiar array of religious practice we've been dealing with along the terraces—the exchange of vices for virtues; the painstaking step-by-step process of rebirth; the prayers and songs and sacred iconography—culminate in something quite new. The language of the church transposes into a startling fusion of spirit and flesh, of piety and passion. "Not a drop of blood is left in me that does not tremble" (30.47), says the pilgrim about the woman who will bring him before God, in whose gaze he will come to see reflected the "splendor of eternal living light" (31.139).

And yet Dante cannot look directly into those unforgettable eyes or marvel at her dazzling smile until he first experiences the sting of her wrath. This comes as a complete surprise. Nothing in the poem has led us to expect Beatrice's fury because all that we have heard about thus far are her "shining, tearful eyes" and "gentle voice," her compassion for his spiritual plight. Not now. She may be his ancient flame, but from her first spoken words—spoken from within the veil but with gloves off—she burns with an icy fire:

"Dante, though Virgil's leaving you, do not
yet weep, do not weep yet; you'll need your tears
for what another sword must yet inflict."

(30.55–57)

There are no signs of welcome or affection from her. Nor will she abide his weeping for Virgil, who departs undetected in the midst of her arrival. Taking no prisoners, Beatrice's tongue is a two-edged sword, and her ferocity astonishing even to her companions, the virtues. Witnessing her fury, they plead for moderation: "Lady, why shame him so?"

We might have assumed once the pilgrim entered Eden that he was beyond such treatment. After all, just moments earlier, Virgil said the pilgrim was free, upright, and whole in his will; that he was crowned and mitred over himself. Apparently not. If Dante's experience is anything to go on, purgatory requires not only a general purification of the sins of the past but a very personal confrontation with those who have been most important to us—inevitably, those we've wronged most. As confrontations go, this one is not pretty. Beatrice rails against Dante's failure to make anything out of what he'd been given. Not only was he richly blessed in talent and opportunity but quite specifically in the gift of her love. Once she died and was no longer in the flesh, he was given dreams and visions and other sorts of inspiration, all intended to lead him back to the true path of Eros which they had charted together. Instead, he lost himself by following a false path. Why?

Given the build-up, the reader expects some epic betrayal or carefully mounted excuse. Instead, the pilgrim answers through his tears, "Present things,/ with their false pleasure, turned my steps aside,/ as soon as your countenance was hidden" (31.34–36). In the intense experience of this particular love, he was shown how to ascend to the sun and the others stars. But once the beloved was gone—and with her, the incentive to persevere—he fell for superficial brightness, fool's gold substitutes for the real thing. He "moved on" and got nowhere: *presenti cose*—"stuff"—got in the way. He forgot what it means to love.

What in the world does this lovers' quarrel in Eden, this fury of a dead woman scorned and the sniveling, if honest, response of a living man—what does any of this have to do with God? And why should a romantic crisis serve as the climactic emotional moment of the *Purgatorio*? I think the answer has to do with the high theological value Dante places on human relationships and, in particular, on the potential of romantic love to lead us to God. One may fall in love with ease but afterwards it is painful and uphill work, as the ascent of the mountain demonstrates terrace after terrace. Working against negative attitudes toward Eros that are as much classical as Christian—that dismiss it as the source of madness, destruction, or the nearest occasion of sin—Dante presents a counter argument through the figure of Beatrice. Human love is not only as strong as death; it is perhaps the most powerful way we can come to know God.

To demonstrate this, Dante forges a dramatic link between Beatrice and Christ that begins in the *Vita nuova* and then flourishes in the *Commedia*. In the moment that initiates the journey, recounted in *Inferno* 2, she descends into hell to bring about Dante's salvation from an infernal dark wood. He remains mindful of her descent into the depths all the way down into the abyss and then again as he spirals upward along the Mountain. At her first appearance to him in purgatory, furthermore, she is greeted by the acclamation that Christ received on the palm-strewn streets of Jerusalem, "*Benedictus qui venis*" (*Purg*. 30.19), "Blessed are you who come." Grammar would demand that Beatrice be "benedicta," but the poet retains the masculine ending of "benedictus" in Latin in order to reinforce the connection between his Lord and this lady. She serves as his Christ-figure, a personal mediator between his own humanity and God's mystery. Dante recognizes this intercession in his final words to her in paradise. This lady, like his Lord, left her footsteps in hell for his salvation, and drew him out of slavery into freedom.

In the *Inferno*, the poet explored Eros as a lethal narcissism through the figure of Francesca. *Amor* is her mantra, the charm that mystifies and misleads. She holds onto her beloved ɪ aolo for eternity, yet what does she really see in him—her silent partner—but a mirror of herself? In Beatrice, however, Dante discovers how love can lead to the Way, the Truth, and the Life. Rather than be a dead end, it can open a door to the most profound reality. According to Charles Williams, whose brilliant theological reading of the *Commedia*, *The Figure of Beatrice*, was of such importance to both Dorothy L. Sayers and W. H. Auden, this trajectory from human to divine was not only what Dante was focused on but essentially what all true love is "up to." "The only question," Williams continues, "is whether lovers are 'up to' Love."[23]

How one learns to be "up to" love is the preoccupation of Dante's purgatory, the realm of the afterlife that is most like earthly existence because, unlike hell and heaven, it entails change, possibility, and the suffering that is bound up in both. Although it presents the "state" of other worldly existence least familiar to Christians who are not Roman Catholic (and then only to Catholics of a certain age), it is nonetheless the most accessible portion of the *Comedy* to relate to—and to appropriate. *Purgatorio* is a poem to live by.

The contrast with *Inferno*, once again, is instructive. Writing about hell gave Dante the chance to present us as stuck, at a loss, trapped in the never-ending compulsion to repeat (rather than transcend) ourselves. It is the nightmare we are lucky to wake up from, and the portion of the larger poem that most people know by reputation if not through actual reading. *Inferno* is the terrible accident on the highway that none of us can pass by without gawking, the horror that we want to turn our back on but cannot. Drawing no doubt upon his own heart of darkness the poet draws us in, holds our attention.

Dante's rendering of purgatory is less compelling, perhaps, but infinitely more useful. It opens up a process whereby what has long been stuck gets loosened, knots are painstakingly (and also pain-fully) untied. Nothing stands still. While hell had its moments of frantic exertion, none of the damned actually gets anywhere. The storm that buffets Paolo and Francesca never relents. Runners in a circle—and there are many throughout the sorrowful kingdom— arrive at no destination. Purgatory, however, presents us with what our three-score-and-ten might look like if we were truly *in via*, on the way toward our best hopes. It offers a liberation theology that can be lived out, not just in some imagined other world but in the middle of the journey of our life. Look carefully at the Mountain's terraces and see what it is like to "get over yourself."

Then there is that climactic scene in the Garden of Eden, where one person looks at another and truth has its day. The tradition teaches us to imagine a frightening end-time Judgment encoun-ter with Christ, which in some sense is what we find when Dante stands in the bracing presence of Beatrice. Yet if the moment is sobering, it is not terrifying. After being in motion the pilgrim comes to a halt. Love confronts him with face unveiled and shows him all of God that can be reflected in human eyes and mouth. The moment is brimful to overflowing. Had we ever imagined that the divine could come this close, could be so bound up with whom— and with how—we love?

All of this theology and poetry is very rich. What happens, however, if someone wants to practice what Dante preaches in the *Purgatorio* but, unlike the pilgrim at the end of his uphill progress, is neither pure nor ready to climb to the stars? In particular, what happens when this vision of Eros runs amuck; when the lovers are alive, in the flesh, and have not yet gone through the process of self-examination and transformation that purgatory entails? In other words, when they are like us?

A perfect example of what can happen when liberation and loose talk about love gets the upper hand is provided by the havoc wreaked on himself and others by none other than Henry Ward Beecher. At the age of almost sixty Beecher was certainly old enough to know better when the crisis broke. Yet no doubt the temptation to lose touch, to become a fool for godly love, was especially strong when, at the height of his career, he was being lionized as the icon of "modern rational religion." Evangelist of a "Gospel of Love," he offered newly liberated Christians the chance to live beyond the old constraints of fear and timidity, to discover "soul affinities" with people to whom they were not related by blood or marriage.[24] Beecher's life went into a meltdown when it turned out that living by his new evangel—and playing with the theological erotic—meant playing with fire.

What does this mean for what Charles Williams spoke of as the "theology of romantic love" celebrated in the *Divine Comedy*? No one can blame Dante for anything that took place in late nineteenth-century Brooklyn. As we have seen, Beecher was no special fan of the poet. Nonetheless, the entire event that gripped America's attention for years in the 1870s can serve as a cautionary tale for anyone who imagines that it is ever easy to be "up to love."

The scandal was in its kindling stage when Beecher first came to New Haven to deliver the inaugural Beecher Lecture in 1871. His biographer refers to this time as the beginning of his descent "into his personal purgatory,"[25] though it is not at all clear whether his ordeal ever led to the rebirth that purgatorial suffering is supposed to yield. In many ways Beecher's crisis was overdue. Throughout his ministry, first in what was then the frontier country of Indiana and subsequently in Brooklyn, there had been various rumors of adultery. There is evidence that Beecher fathered at least one "love child" apart from the legitimate ten he had with his woefully neglected wife, Eunice.[26] All of this caught up with him, however, when newspaperman Theodore Tilton began more and more openly to charge that his celebrity-pastor and former friend was a master of infidelity, a wolf in clergyman's clothing. "I am reliably assured," said Tilton, "that Beecher preaches to seven or eight of his mistresses every Sunday evening." The press of the time, as in our own, loved this sort of thing: clerical indiscretions are always welcome news. Not surprisingly, the number of reputed mistresses in the pews grew with every retelling—from "seven or eight," to a dozen, to forty.

Tilton was not only outraged as a Plymouth Church parishioner. He also spoke as a husband who believed Beecher had stolen his wife Elizabeth's affections, played on her sympathies by complaining about his own unhappy marriage, and bewitched her with pious talk. He "took advantage of her orthodox views to make [them] the net and mesh in which he ensnared her." More than lust, in other words, it was religion that was the root of the affair. "They were years courting each other by mutual piety," Tilton maintained, with Beecher assuring the gullible Elizabeth that God would never blame them for what was, after all, a "high, religious love." Theirs was a passion rooted in "companionship of mind" and the Christian "gospel of love," which soared above both the vulgar and the conventional. According to Elizabeth, their intimacy was as "natural and sincere an expression of love as words of endearment."²⁷ She knew herself to be spotless and chaste, as indeed her pastor repeatedly told her she was. He also insisted that they need keep the relationship a secret lest lower minds poison what was so beautiful. Mrs. Tilton suffered from this subterfuge, which Beecher (referring to one of his novels) preferred to look upon as "*nest-hiding.*"²⁸

Of course, with people as relentlessly self-dramatizing as this group—not to mention their presence forever in the public eye—nothing remained hidden very long. Nor was anyone involved left unscarred. In-house or front-stoop gossip circulated widely and quickly turned into print, with accusations that Plymouth Church, epicenter of it all, was a hotbed of free love. Victoria Woodhull and her "free-love suffragettes" broke the story. Compromising letters were hidden and then handed around. Copious tears were shed during impassioned interviews and charges either believed or dismissed by people who felt they needed to take sides. Even the Beecher family was a house divided, with sisters Catherine Beecher, Isabella Beecher Hooker, and Harriet Beecher Stowe variously accusing and defending their brother.

All of this was coming to a boil during the same years, 1871–1874, when Beecher made his regular way to New Haven to deliver the lectures dedicated to the memory of his dour father. Only a year after his final lecture, in 1875, *Theodore Tilton v. Henry Ward Beecher, Action for Criminal Conversation* was tried in Brooklyn Civil Court.[29] It instantly fostered a media frenzy the likes of which some of us remember from 1995's televised O. J. Simpson trial. In the end, the jury would be unable to reach a verdict and the case was dropped. Nothing about the circumstances or those involved stood beyond doubt. Beecher exited the courthouse victorious, yet left behind him a compromised reputation and a wake of ruined lives. What actually took place, adultery in the heart or between the sheets? Historians remain unclear about what transpired between him and Elizabeth Tilton, or with the "seven or eight" or dozen or forty women in Plymouth Church who allegedly were his mistresses. No one knows for sure if the "gospel of love" ever went from push to shove.

There is no hint of this turmoil in the transcripts of Beecher's published *Yale Lectures on Preaching*, yet one has only to read his letters from this period to learn the cost of the seemingly endless controversy. Not only was his vocation at stake but the public adulation he craved—which may well have meant more to him than truth. He confided to Frank Moulton, a once-trusted friend:

Nothing can possibly be so bad as the horror of the great darkness, in which I spend much of my time. I look upon death as sweeter faced than any friend I have in the world. Life would be pleasant if I could see that rebuilt which is shattered; but to live on the sharp and ragged edge of anxiety, remorse, fear, despair, and yet to put on all the appearances of serenity and happiness, cannot be endured much longer.[30]

Yet for all this, Beecher's public composure, both in church and in the courtroom, was sure. The Plymouth congregation not only embraced him but raised his already princely annual salary of $20,000 to $100,000 to help defray expenses he'd incurred during the trial. Until his death in 1887, he kept up a full schedule of preaching, writing, and lecturing at home and abroad. He championed the theory of evolution and continued to throw himself into political controversy and notoriety—a lifetime predilection.

In Brooklyn's Greenwood Cemetery the biblical epitaph inscribed on his tombstone reads, "He Thinketh No Evil." It represents a curious adjustment of the Scripture, a surprising switch of subject to himself —"He thinketh"—and therefore away from the virtue celebrated by St. Paul in 1 Corinthians 13:5, where we are told (in the language of the King James Version) that it is charity that "doth not behave itself unseemly, seeketh not her own, is not easily provoked, thinketh no evil." Beecher interchangeable with *caritas*?

I wonder if whoever chose this edited fragment of the Pauline verse did so with any sense of irony or somehow forgot the unseemly behavior and self-seeking of a lifetime. No one in Beecher's day did more to popularize the notion of God as lover or to develop the expectation that the preacher should be a star. Yet when it came to individual people rather than crowds, there were probably few who were less adept, less "up to" love, than he.

So where is he now, this brilliant, curious soul among the ragamuffin communion of saints? None of us can say. But if there is a purgatory, and if it is anything like the one Dante imagined spiraling its way up the seven-story mountain, then Brother Henry is no doubt in the blessed company of redeemed sinners all diligently working out their own salvation. Is he on the terrace of pride, shouldering his immense, hungry ego, or among the wrathful making recompense for all those he maligned? Is he groaning along with the avaricious for hoarding his reputation, that idealization of himself which became his personal mammon? Given that it is now some 120 years after his death, might he have moved closer to the Garden of Eden, where God knows what Beatrice may be waiting to read him the riot act? Or might he be presently running along the fiery terrace of lust, whose flames burn away all the nonsense that has been thought, spoken, or done in the name of love, and perhaps especially by the golden-tongued—all of them discovering that most of what they wrote was at best a partial truth, at worst balderdash?

How quickly the idealized story of Dante and Beatrice can devolve into the reality of the Reverend Beecher and Mrs. Tilton. How little it takes for a stark truth to turn into emotional fog, or for what we blindly imagine to be our virtues appear as vices once they come to light. The *Purgatorio* asks us to imagine a place in the afterlife where such revelations dawn over a period of otherworld time, for as long as it takes. The burden of the poem, however, has to do with the way we live now. The goal is to learn how to be "up to love" no matter how painful the lesson. But why wait for the world to come?

O, More than That . . .
Much More than That

PARADISE

Today, almost anyone with the requisite fifteen minutes of fame ends up on *Larry King Live*. On July 19, 2007, it happened to be her turn: Tammy Faye Bakker. I had followed her career since March 1987, when the dean of the Yale Divinity School sent me to Heritage, USA, the epicenter of the then-thriving PTL ("Praise the Lord") Club. I was there to investigate contemporary Christian communication among the media savvy—people not like me or anyone I knew. First stop had been Pat Robertson's CBN University, with its apocalyptic fervor and scary politics. I could not wait to leave. By contrast, Heritage was an inviting "People That Love" resort with a shopping mall, Goody Barn, water park, and high-rise hotel. The crowds who traveled there expected a Christian Disney World and seemed to find exactly what they sought. More than one happy camper described it as "a little bit of heaven on earth."

Yet for all the fun, I happened to arrive when there was trouble in paradise. It was the very day when Tammy Faye's prescription drug addiction and her residence at the Betty Ford Center were both disclosed for the first time. In a matter of weeks one scandal led to another. The empire quickly crumbled, and the woman who formerly seemed always to cry at the drop of a hat now had every reason to keep the mascara running. After a subsequent career on television that culminated in her appearance on a reality show, *The Surreal Life*, she kept making lemonade from the lemons life gave her—a laugh line that became her theme song. Against my better judgment, I liked her.

The Tammy Faye interviewed by Larry King was not going live for the first time, but certainly no one had ever seen her like this before. The makeup was still thick, the dress bright red, her jewelry as gaudy as ever, but since 1994 an inoperable cancer had taken its terrible toll on her colon, lungs, and spine. At sixty-five pounds, with her showbiz belter's voice reduced to a high whisper, she was clearly at the end of her life. In fact, just two days after the broadcast, she died.

It came as no surprise that the interview stayed close to religion, and not only because of her ravaged state. This was Tammy Faye, after all, who had always been ready to give an account of the faith that was in her. Furthermore, she was in the hands of Larry King, a Jewish agnostic married to a pious Mormon, who knows his television audience very well. According to a Gallup poll taken in May 2007, roughly nine in ten Americans believe in God and almost as many (81 percent) in heaven.[31] His viewers, therefore, would want to know how this weepy but unfailingly upbeat woman, whose life and celebrity had been defined by her exuberant Christianity, was facing her end.

The interview included the clowning that everyone expected of Tammy Faye. In answer to the question, "How do you want to be remembered?" she replied, "For my eyelashes." But much of the talk revolved around the afterlife. Pointing her finger upward, she told Larry, "I know where I'm headed . . . I believe when I leave the earth, because I love the Lord, I am going straight to heaven." No purgatory for her! When asked to speak directly to her fans, she told them, "I genuinely want to see you in heaven someday." Later on in the program, Larry King asked her new-style evangelist son, Jamie Bakker, to define his mother's sure and certain hope. Heaven, he said, "is where God lives. It's where we have no more pain and suffering. And we're able to be with the Creator."[32] On the day after her death, Jim Bakker, her former husband and PTL co-host, elaborated further. Tammy Faye "is now in heaven with her mother and grandmother and Jesus Christ. . . ."[33] This was, he said, the comfort he could give to all who loved her. Had he preached at her funeral, he would no doubt have said that heaven is up above, that it is the "presence of God," and that it includes encounters with the five people (or, in Tammy Faye's case, maybe thousands) you would really want to meet there.

Funerals, and the deathbeds that lead up to them, inevitably force even the most hesitant among us to say something about heaven. This is especially the case for clergy. After all, part of the minister's job is to comfort and encourage the faithful when they've dwindled to sixty-five pounds and can barely speak. They do not want to be told that their pastor does not have a clue, even if that is the God's-honest truth. They want to know what, if anything, they have to hold onto when everything is slipping away. Once *they* have slipped away, there will be time to intone the appropriate psalms, speak of the many mansions in the Father's house, and conjure up that new heaven and new earth where "Death will be no more; mourning and crying and pain will be no more" (Rev 21:4). But as long as the dying are still alive, they will want something less secondhand and roundabout than stock biblical assurances, however valuable they may be. "Preacher, what's next?"

Scripture, as we've noted, is reticent about such matters. The prophet Samuel is brought back momentarily from the netherworld of Sheol, where all the dead make their way in shadows (1 Sam 28). Jesus certainly discourages thoughts of ongoing family ties in heaven ("they neither marry nor are given in marriage," Mark 12:25), and Paul speaks in 1 Corinthians 15 of a spiritual resurrection body that is barely imaginable. Not that many haven't tried: in the *City of God* Augustine imagined our heavenly bodies to be gorgeously thirty-something, the same age as Christ; for Origen they would most likely be spherical in shape. Brief moments in Ezekiel, Daniel, the Book of Enoch, and the Revelation according to John variously paint a composite picture of the celestial paradise that tradition has celebrated for more than two millennia. What does heaven look like? On the one hand, it has a throne, a divinity who sits upon it, and on every side a concert of continuous praise; on the other, it is a jeweled cube as radiant as a bride, in which Eden's paradise and Jerusalem's holy city join in one perfect place where God reigns eternally. Add to this angels and incense, elders and crowns, crystal rivers, trees in perpetual fruit, and four living creatures (their wings emblazoned with eyes)—all of this converging as a cry goes up, "Holy, holy, holy, the Lord God the Almighty, who was and is and is to come" (Rev 4:8). "There we shall be still and we shall see," says Augustine in a daisy-chain of promises, "we shall see and we shall love; we shall love and we shall praise." Or, as Peter Abelard wrote in the twelfth century and John Mason Neale translated in the mid-nineteenth,

> O what their joy and their glory must be,
> those endless Sabbaths the blessed ones see;
> crown for the valiant, to weary ones rest;
> God shall be All, and in all shall be blest.[34]

This vision of a universal convergence on God and God alone is predominantly how Christians have conceived of heaven, at least "officially." The redeemed creation draws together around a divine center in whom every wheel-spoke finds its place, who is the divine All in which the blessed discover their "all in all." What this might mean, of course, has been construed differently over the centuries. For Origen and other fathers of the Eastern church, the Pauline phrase from 1 Corinthians 15:28, "that God may be all in all," pointed to an ultimate reintegration, an *apocatastasis*, when no creature, not even Satan, would be able to resist the draw of the Logos. This optimism was not to be the way of the Christian West, which concocted the notion—thanks to a terrible passage in Augustine[35]—that one aspect of celestial joy would be the saints' contemplation of God's punishment of the damned.

Thankfully, this idea, though also taken up by others, was never more than a ghastly sideline. For Aquinas, heaven was to be understood primarily as an uninterrupted act of divine contemplation. For all eternity the redeemed would know God fully, without mediation, and each according to his or her individual capacity. The blessed would find their true selves by being lost in the wonder, love, and praise of the Trinity. Moreover, despite the plenitude of angels, archangels and all the company of heaven, the blessed would discover their bliss essentially one-on-One. "If there were but a single soul enjoying God," Aquinas argued hypothetically in the *Summa*, "it would be happy, though having no neighbor to love."

Other theologians emphasized the corporate, social dimension of beatitude. Even in his most Neo-Platonic "alone-to-the-Alone" phase, Augustine's famous post-conversion rapture to heaven— when he reached out and, for a heartbeat, "touched" the divine presence—was not, in fact, undertaken on his own, but in the company of Monica. Mother and son were talking about "those endless Sabbaths the blessed ones see" when suddenly the conversation took off—literally.

It comes as no surprise, then, that Augustine presents beatitude as a shared mystery in the final book of his magnum opus on divine civility, the *City of God*. How do the redeemed see God "face to face"? He readily admits that there can be no definitive answer to this question, but perhaps God will be known and visible to us when we behold each other. The blessed will see God, in other words, by looking around.

But what about Mom and Grandma, or a lost partner, a child, a friend—people who are hard to live without right now, and without whom eternity would seem less than blessed? Do these attachments continue in the eternal communion of saints, so that in heaven we enjoy a succession of reunions? Augustine gives credence to this notion in his *Confessions* when he asks his readers to pray for the souls of his parents. Monica and Patricius remain, even after their passing, his "kith and kin" in the Lord. Yet he also suggests that in glory the couple, who were highly fraught as parents, will become something like low-impact siblings, less parents than fellow citizens of heaven. In a letter to a grieving widow, Italica, Augustine gives her reason to hope, though not by promising an afterlife embrace with her spouse. That will be the stuff of nineteenth-century imaginings, Latter-Day Saint revelation, and Mitch Albom's ongoing best-seller, *The Five People You Meet in Heaven*. Instead, Augustine offers a more general consolation. The dead have not been lost; rather, they have entered a life that we too will share, when our beloveds will be even dearer to us than they once were because in glory we will know them better. Nor will there be any of the anxiety about loss or change that haunts all earthly affections. In paradise, loving is forever.

Other theologians go further in arguing for the sociability of heaven. Giles of Rome, a student of Thomas Aquinas, said that the blessed will speak to one another freely and in audible language, not because they need to know anything but out of the sheer pleasure of conversing. Since conversation is a social solace in this life, why should it not continue in the age to come? And why should one not be able to talk to everyone with pleasure? Along these lines, Bonaventure says that in heaven there will be no such thing as a stranger or mere acquaintance. Everyone will be a new best friend, so that whoever now seems to be remote or standoffish will hereafter be a nearest and dearest: "Love will then be extended to all the saints in a way which was possible only toward one single dearest friend." Yet marriage will have no place; neither will there be any private creaturely affections to distract from the Big One. Without effort, love will delight to stay on task.

By the Renaissance, this theocentrism began to lose its appeal. In the fifteenth-century paintings of paradise by Fra Angelico and Giovanni di Paolo, for instance, the blessed are to be seen not only ranked before the throne of God but also dancing elegantly with one another, embracing and kissing, sometimes in intense pairs, sometimes in threesomes. Later, Jonathan Edwards asks his parishioners to expect many such recognition scenes: with the dead infant, the father and mother, husband or wife, the friend — and not only those already known personally but also "the patriarchs and fathers and saints of the Old and New Testaments . . . with whom on earth we were only conversant by faith." By the nineteenth century, when there was ideally a maternal angel at the hub of every middle-class home, the heavenly Jerusalem took on the distinctly "cozy" feel of a Currier and Ives print. In the most sentimental of these heavenly expectations we are almost in the world of fifties television when Dad comes back at the end of the day, sticks his head in the door with a smile, and cries out, "Honey, I'm home!"

In this domestic scenario, Mom and Grandma can easily be found around the heavenly hearth, but where is Jesus Christ? The presence of God fades as the apotheosis of domesticity takes its place. Staying within the nuclear family replaces celestial citizenship as a goal. Even passionate romance between soul mates, explored by the love poets of the Middle Ages, is at last given an endless green light. To fall in love, as the cliché would have it, is to "die and go to heaven." For Dante, as we have seen, the mutually-besotted find their place in hell. Not so, according to Emily Dickinson—the beatific vision *is* the lover's gaze:

> The "Life that is" will then have been
> A thing I never knew—
> As Paradise fictitious
> Until the Realm of you—
>
> The "Life that is to be," to me
> A Residence too plain
> Unless in my Redeemer's Face
> I recognize your own—"[36]

Perhaps Emanuel Swedenborg first caught this tide at the end of the eighteenth century when his celestial visions revealed something other than God as "all in all." There would indeed be marriage in heaven, and sex, as well as cities, orchards, and gardens—our world, but in its perfected state. Swedenborg rejected the static ideal of eternal rest, contemplation and praise, which to his mind amounted to idleness and sloth: we'd all be bored silly. Rather, the blessed in their newly angelic condition would continue to practice old virtues in their new capacity as citizens of heaven. Instead of resting in God they would work on his behalf, and enjoy doing so; they would also make spiritual progress. It would be forever onward and upward!

It would also be, according to Elizabeth Stuart Phelps' immensely popular *The Gates Ajar* (1868), all about *us*. Gone is the old belief that heaven is "all to do with harps, adoration, and learning something about the nature of God." Instead it is about family, and better homes and gardens. Aunt Winifred, the novel's central character and spokesperson for the author, expects "to have my beautiful home, and my husband and [child] as I had them here; with many differences and great ones, but mine just the same."[37] The "life that is to be," come the kingdom, will be in heaven as it is on earth, though much improved.

Take away the visionary specifics of Swedenborg's Church of the New Jerusalem (cut back on the angels), then trim *The Gates Ajar* of its domestic excesses, and what you probably get is the heaven that 81 percent of Americans believe in — a better version of what we already know and treasure. There's Mom and Grandma, and Jesus Christ, perhaps, at his most benign. But what matters above all is that none of what we have loved about this life has been lost, including the sensuous beauties of the earth and — who knows? — that tiger cat purring in your lap or the puppy catching a Frisbee midair. All of what we've loved is still here, somewhere, and better than ever.

Along these lines, I think of a passage in Marilynne Robinson's 2004 novel, *Gilead*. It is an exchange between two elderly ministers, one of them, John Boughton, very close to his death. What we read is reported to us by John Ames, the diarist-narrator who writes the story of his life for a young son he will not see into adulthood.

Boughton says he has more ideas about heaven every day. He said, "Mainly I just think about the splendors of the world and multiply by two. I'd multiply by ten or twelve if I had the energy. But two is much more than sufficient for my purposes." So he's just sitting there multiplying the feel of the wind by two, multiplying the smell of grass by two. "I remember when we put that old wagon on the court-house roof,'" he said. "Seems to me the stars were brighter in those days. Twice as bright."

"And we were twice as clever."

"O, more than that," he said. "Much more than that."

Would either of these septuagenarian ministers actually have preached that "the best pleasure of this world" constituted heaven? Probably not, even though Ames thinks that his dying friend was not far off track in thinking so. The sentiment to which he actually awards an Amen is summed up in a couple of lines by Isaac Watts: "Grant me on earth what seems Thee best,/ Till Death and Heav'n reveal the rest."[38] One can easily imagine these verses as a punch line for a latter-day Calvinist preacher who, like his Reformation mentor, did not want to encourage "curious speculations" about the unknowable. Death and heaven will reveal what is to be in the Lord's own good time, so let's leave well enough alone and avoid the Land of Cockaigne and the Big Rock Candy Mountain.

Who could quarrel with this position? It's sensible, safe, and cannot lead anyone astray. There's also nothing self-indulgent or fantasized about it, which is so often the case when it comes to thinking about heaven. But I wonder what would happen if a Boughton or an Ames mounted the pulpit and, after turning on the lectern light and clearing his throat, spoke what he felt and not what he ought to say? Might they tell their congregations that the life-in-God, which heaven finally comes down to, is already with us (to recall poet Franz Wright's phrase) in "the holiness of things/ precisely as they are"[39]—in the feel of the wind and the smell of grass, the brightness of stars, and the conversational give-and-take between old friends—and perhaps most deeply in the best instances of our loving? If so, preachers would be urging the people in the pews to allow their experience here and now to open up, to blossom into wonder. What if they asked their congregations to bless the moment, fan it like a coal, and let its light lead them higher up and further in, beyond even the greatest expectations that have come to mind; to lead them to whatever it is that God has in store for them in the very next moment or even in the one that follows upon their final breath—to the divine "whatever" that has always been one of the Lord's best kept secrets? What if a preacher like Ames dared to say, and not in a private diary, but in the pulpit, that the deep joy of looking into the face of his wife or of his young son is but the first installment of an ultimate face-to-face vision already implicit in the ones we now cherish?

I focus on preachers here in part because of Robinson's novel, in part because, when it comes to imagining the undiscovered country, clergy are held responsible for having something to say. Like it or not, they are expected to be professionals of what comes next. The rest of us are free of this burden. No one demands that we have an insight or an inspiring word. It is enough to be spiritual, not religious—to shrug our shoulders and say, good naturedly, "Frankly, I have no idea." Still, clergy are not the only ones privy to the dying, or to the questions of the young who want to know what happened to Grandma now that she has stopped showing up at 4 o'clock to make tea. We watch Tammy Faye on *Larry King Live*, hear her talk with utter confidence about her imminent departure from this life, and wonder about what we would feel or look forward to if we were in her shoes—as one day we will be. We also, increasingly as time goes by, wonder if this life is a preparation for any other, or if what has begun to grow in us might flower in some other dimension. All bets are off, there's no telling, it is all conjecture—but what if?

Heaven has been studied at length, anthologized, and taken up anew in our own day (on the Internet and elsewhere) in inverse proportion to the time spent on it in church. In my experience preachers stay away from it like the plague, no doubt because so much of what we have heard over the years is sentimental or downright cheesy. (I like Mark Twain's characterization of Mrs. Phelps' other world in *The Gates Ajar* as "a mean little ten-cent heaven about the size of Rhode Island.")

We do not have any direct revelations from Dante as to what he thought of contemporary talk about paradise. I fancy, however, that he was not enthralled with what he heard from priests in Florence or in the other cities he lived in while writing the *Divine Comedy.* All indications are that he was a highly critical layman with no truck for lazy or incompetent clergy. The *Comedy* was not only his letter to the world but also his sermon, and one that takes more than a few pot shots at the clerical preaching of his own day. In *Paradiso* 29, for instance, Beatrice holds forth on the nonsense that frequently pours forth from men with clerical stoles around their necks. She calls it fables, trash, jests and buffoonery, outright folly. Pulpit professionals offer a travesty of the mission entrusted to the apostles and passed down within the church. She tells the pilgrim, "Christ did not say to his first company,/ 'Go, and preach idle stories to the world';/ but he gave them the true foundation" (*Par.* 29.109–111). In place of Scripture the "new disciples" proclaim gossip and chatter, tell stories about St. Anthony's pig, or entertain pointless theories about the eclipse that darkened the earth at Christ's death. Given this adulteration of the Word, the pulpit may be an unlikely place to hear Scripture proclaimed.

Or so Dante seems to suggest by offering us his own poetic proclamation of the Word of God. In his exploration of the afterlife, we discover our earthly existence seen in the imagined light of God's judgment. Dante took the Tuscan world of the early fourteenth century and revealed that, when opened up, it could give a foretaste of eternity. What the pilgrim finds over the course of his journey is that that the affections and hatreds of earth continue to rage in hell. Purgatory is a very intense version of what Christian life on earth should be all about. And the ascent into heaven begins with an act as simple as a man looking into the face of the woman who first opened his heart and eyes when they were both only children.

Furthermore, his journey is a massive series of reunions, most spectacularly, as we have seen, with Beatrice, but also with friends he once had, enemies who still bring his blood to a boil, a couple of relatives (one in hell, one in paradise), and a slew of figures he'd only read or heard about—Virgil first among them. In short, while Dante's afterlife takes place in the life to come, it is by no means foreign to the here and now. We anticipate hell in Pisa's Tower of Hunger when the door is nailed shut and Ugolino's starving children cry out for food. We also recognize the splendor of heaven when a human face, like that of Beatrice, suddenly becomes resplendent with luminosity beyond its own. The poet takes our world through the looking glass, to the rear of the wardrobe, not just because he can only write about what he knows but because he believes that *this* is the beginning of *that*. Now we see in a glass, darkly; then, we will see light in light. As the Psalmist has it, "For with you is the fountain of life; in your light we see light" (36:9).

Despite Dante's claim to have been there ("I was in the heaven that most receives his light," 1.4–5), he, like everyone else, is making it up as he goes along, bringing out of his treasure, like the householder in Jesus' parable, "what is new and what is old" (Matt 13:52). Nonetheless, like the simulacrum of divinity that Ezekiel sees at the beginning of his prophecy, *Paradiso* gives us a vision of the likeness of the glory of God. It may be only a facsimile of a facsimile, not the real thing, but it can get you longing for what it cannot give.

Psalm 36's notion of seeing light in light is as good a way as any to describe the *Comedy*'s third and final canticle. Its subject is the heavenly Jerusalem, the City of God Dante believed to be located in the highest reach of heaven, which the ancients believed to be full of immaterial light, and thus in another dimension from our own—off the map, wholly beyond the reach of time and space. The pilgrim journeys there by gradually ascending through the nine material heavens, which are interlocking crystalline spheres holding the planets and stars: the Moon, Mercury, Venus, the Sun, Mars, Jupiter, Saturn, and the Fixed Stars. Sweeping the whole structure along is the Primum Mobile, the ninth heaven and outermost skin of the material world. At the core of this concentric universe stands the immobile earth while around it dance the nine celestial spheres, each one governed by a different order of angels, each whirling at a different speed, all orchestrated in a cosmic dance. From the perspective of our black holes and sense of limitless outer space, such a notion of the beyond may appear incredibly tiny and enclosed—the spheres like Russian dolls, one snugly tucked inside the other. With its greater capacity for mystery and awe, however, Dante's age might well be better at celebrating what we (rather than they) can actually see, thanks to the far sight of the Hubble telescope. Behold the wonder: starbursts in astonishing color, galaxies and nebulae, swirls of light, a plumy eagle.

In order to prepare the pilgrim for his vision of God "face to face," and to share with him the beatific vision of the Trinity, the blessed beam themselves down to appear in the successive material heavens. We see them in their star power, either as individual flames or as constellations of light in various symbolic formations. Once Dante arrives in the Empyrean, or tenth heaven, he receives a special dispensation in line with all the others he has been given thus far. He beholds the blessed in the bodies they will have at the end of time, after the general resurrection of the dead. Whereas *Paradiso* had been all in motion until now, the Empyrean shows the blessed sitting still in the round, higher or lower depending on their spiritual "size place," in a hierarchy that Dante believed to be fundamental to existence. Arranged in the shape of a white rose whose petals extend upward from a vast golden center, the blessed contemplate God, love to the capacity of their vision, and shine with corresponding ardor. It is at the heart of this "eternal rose" that the pilgrim experiences his own contemplative moment, the vision that was the goal of the journey from the beginning even as it is the fixed aim of all rational creation, angelic as well as human. What we find in the end is a synthesis of the theocentric and the social. The blessed find their places among one another. But all look up together to behold the "eternal fountain," the common source that fills each to capacity forever.

If only the poet could cope! Words fail him, and despite the stunning achievement of *Paradiso* Dante presents his vision as always, and at most, the next best thing. He is openly aware of the challenge he is up against—the vision of God and of realities that cannot be spoken about easily or perhaps at all—and tells us so at the outset. *Paradiso's* vision cannot be put into language adequately; it is bound to disappoint. Nonetheless, the little that the poet can remember and verbalize, he *will* set down—and in words that leave all the other contenders behind in the dust.

It has to be said, however, that most readers of the third canticle are not entirely ecstatic over the result. They miss the excitement of *Inferno* and the sense of becoming new that is found in *Purgatorio*—in other words, miss the poignant encounters with lost souls or with those who are works-in-progress like us. Even Dante diehards understand the problem: *Paradiso* does not start off invitingly. The poet seems to take this into account in the address to his readers that opens canto two. Those interested only in smooth sailing had better turn back now. There are rough seas ahead, not to mention stretches of ocean that seem like the deadest calm. Only the strong of heart should continue.

The first third of the *Paradiso* gives us a series of theological questions meticulously answered in the manner of the Scholastic masters, which only leads to a new crop of questions springing up. People not taking a Dante course frequently jump ship at this point in their reading. But no matter how difficult the start-up, the reader, like the pilgrim, needs to realize that we are in the process of regaining the "good of the intellect" (*Inf.* 3.18) which had been lost in hell, retrieved in purgatory, and is now ready for a rigorous work-out—or what's a heaven for? The pilgrim is meant to ask questions, and also to see that answers generate more inquiry. It is *good* to know, to exercise the intellect. Indeed, it should be a joy to do so.

Furthermore, Dante has his work cut out for him at the outset. There are *Paradiso* ground rules that need to be established before taking on beatitude. Among the most difficult of these is the issue of hierarchy that arises early on when Dante meets a female member of the powerful Florentine Donati clan. For Piccarda's presence in the slowest and therefore lowest of the heavenly spheres disturbs him. She seems to be at the greatest remove from the highest reach of heaven and therefore, in some sense, at the farthest remove from God. Understanding his dismay, she smiles, as do so many of the blessed, before explaining that she is perfectly content with the spiritual station that her momentary appearance in the Moon betokens. Her placement is the will of God, "and in his will is our peace" (3.85). What's not to love?

Dante understands these words perfectly well: "every place/ in Heaven is in Paradise," he says, "though grace/ does not rain equally from the High Good" (vv. 88–90). But this does not mean that he likes what he hears anymore than do most present-day readers. Beatrice honors his problem over the "unfairness" of hierarchy when she assures him that in paradise God "rains" so abundantly upon each of the blessed that they are each full to overflowing. Moreover, apart from this command performance for Dante's sake, every one of the blessed is forever and always *in* the highest heaven. They only appear to him in the lower spheres to signify their spiritual "size place." In reality, each cup is full to overflowing. The fact that some cups are larger than others—that the demitasse, although filled to the brim, holds less than the tankard—means only that different capacities of spirit, as opposed to an identical capacity for beatitude, is part of the divine plan. The "volume" of each human vessel is the product first of God's gift to the individual and then of his or her meritorious realization of that gift. In heaven, each soul is always at capacity.

In our world, as National Public Radio's Garrison Keillor jokes of his fictional Lake Wobegon, "all the children are above average"; in the same spirit, a certain Boston private school advertises itself as a place where "all our students are leaders." Dante would not only think this a lie but a nightmare. For him, difference was hard-wired into the nature of things. We are reminded of this frequently in *Paradiso*, and not only by Beatrice. No less a personage than the Emperor Justinian speaks out in favor of "difference," an affirmative action of the spirit, while the Dominican Thomas and the Franciscan Bonaventure put aside their rivalries for a time to acknowledge that the church has been well served by the strikingly different gifts of "the one and the other," by Francis's heart and Dominic's brain.

The sticking point here is probably not the notion of "the one and the other," or of the variety of gifts that are all necessary for a community to flourish, as St. Paul wrote to the quarrelsome Corinthians. It is not enough that Beatrice reassures us that there is not a bad seat in all of heaven and that everyone thrills to the music of the spheres. What rankles is that some who listen take in more, have a deeper connection to the music, and "get it" at a more profound level. This is not just because, so to speak, they practiced the piano more diligently during their life (which is not difficult to accept). It is because God gave them their extraordinary gift out of an inscrutable desire to do so. Not fair? Only if you have decided that it must be otherwise, that everyone must be the same. Dante sees the variability of human gifts ultimately as God's business, not our own. What one of us cannot know or see so fully, another can—a fact that in *Paradiso* inspires not a sullen frown but a radiant smile.

None of this is Dante's invention. Heaven's equal partnership among unequals, its celebration of unity amid difference, is articulated quite beautifully by Augustine at the end of the *City of God*, whose authority Dante is probably following in this matter. The passage in question follows upon Augustine's observation that there will be different degrees of merit in heaven, the very thing that appeals neither to the pilgrim nor to us: "No one will want what he does not have; he'll be bound in closest harmony with one to whom it has been granted. And so although one will have a gift inferior to another, he will also have the compensatory gift of contentment with what he has." The goal is equal affection, joint ownership—not uniformity.

The ideal of partnership, first introduced as the constitutive principle of heaven in *Purgatorio* 15, achieves fullness in *Paradiso*. This is as it should be, given the nature of God as a partner in himself, God's unity being composed of the mutual loving of three divine persons. Because partnership is God's own truth, it comes as no surprise to see it also expressed among the blessed. When the pilgrim approaches the sphere of Mercury, for instance, each of the souls declares, as if overjoyed at the approach of a new partner in God, "Here now is one who will increase our loves!" (5.104). In the heaven of Jupiter, moreover, the individual blessed appear in the collective form of an eagle, "uttering with its voice both *I* and *mine*/ when *we* and *ours* were what, in thought, were meant" (19.11–12). Because they are all rooted in God, their center and circumference, the blessed can also see into one another fully. They are of one mind and heart—and the more the merrier.

The discrepancy between their shared omniscience and Dante's limited earthly understanding causes the pilgrim some frustration. He complains to one of the souls, who surely knows his question even before he poses it, "I would not have to wait for your request/ if I could enter you as you do me" (9.80–81). This English translation of the Italian, "s'io m'intuassi, come tu t'inmii" is adequate enough, but the line deserves a more literal rendering. For what the pilgrim does is employ an odd, made-up language to dramatize the immediacy (not to mention the intimacy) of communication among the blessed. Dante says to the soul, "If only I in-you-ed myself, as you in-me yourself." This same sense of radical inter-subjectivity, of I in you and you in me, is found throughout the canticle whenever the poet constructs new reflexive verbs out of nouns and pronouns. One can in-pearl oneself, find oneself to be in-sapphire, in-future, in-eternity, in-her, in-him, in-paradise, and in-God. Heaven's reality requires a new-minted heavenspeak to do it justice, a "transhumanization" of our language to suggest a barely conceivable communion.

To an extent unparalleled by any other visionary text, language itself is part of *Paradiso*'s theological adventure. Dante would have us believe that he is always at a loss for the right word, and again and again pronounces his failure as a poet. It is easy to dismiss these protestations as signs of bad faith on his part. Surely he must have realized he succeeded brilliantly at writing on water, in capturing the ephemeral shimmer of light before it darkens or changes into another kind of shine. But perhaps because he realized all that he could *not* say, his protestations are not coy but, rather, honest admissions. After all, can anyone truly "succeed" when describing light, love, or God?

A sense of failure and loss is inevitable when approaching God. And so, over the course of the *Paradiso* an image will last as long as a bubble before bursting into airy nothing. A lengthy description will collapse just after being very exactly constructed, when the poet in effect tells us, "That's not what I meant, that's not what I meant at all." Perhaps the most a writer burdened by such a project can do is hope that at least a trace of the experience will be left behind, the trajectory of a misfired metaphor — *something* understood.

By the beginning of the *Commedia*'s hundredth canto, the circle that opened up in *Inferno* 1 draws to its close. St. Bernard of Clairvaux, the pilgrim's final guide, entrusts him to the Virgin Mary, whose intervention on his behalf first sent Beatrice to Virgil and Virgil to the "dark wood." Bernard's intercessory prayer fills the Virgin with delight, and so she, like Beatrice before her, turns her face upward with a smile. Dante does not need to be told to do likewise. He effortlessly follows the drift, borne aloft on a tide no sailor in his right mind would want to resist.

From this point on, the poet alternates between avowals of
what he cannot say and remembered fragments of what he saw.
First, the whole of the universe like a million scattered pages seems
brought together and bound by love into one volume. Then, that
"book" becomes three circles of the same dimension but of distinct coloration. Finally, within the central circle, at the heart of
the Trinity, he sees Christ, the human form of the One who looks
like us but who made us in his divine image and likeness.

Even at this eleventh hour of the journey, the knottiest doctri-
nal questions come flooding. How can God be three and one, or
Christ be the Word made flesh? The pilgrim struggles to rational-
ize mysteries—Trinity, Incarnation—that cannot be disentangled
even by genius. What is he like in this quandary? A frustrated
student of geometry comes to the poet's mind, someone hopelessly
intent on squaring the circle and always coming up short. The task
cannot be done:

> As the geometer intently seeks
> to square the circle, but he cannot reach,
> through thought on thought, the principle he needs,
> so I searched that strange sight: I wished to see
> the way in which our human effigy
> suited the circle and found a place in it
> —but my own wings were far too weak for that.
>
> (33.133–139)

The Italian word for wings, *penne*, is also the word for pens, so
that Dante is here making a double confession of failure, as both a
visionary and a writer. He cannot reach his goal, but then he does
not have to. Experience overwhelms the rational mind, and the pilgrim finds himself transported into the reality of God by the love

that moves the sun and the other stars. As the poet then falls into silence, we arrive at the resonant failure of the poem's magnificent close. Dante has set the stage, created the longing to know how the story turns out, but the face-to-face encounter remains a mystery yet to be revealed. The reader is left (purposefully, I think) with a hunger and thirst for glory.

For some of us, this hunger and thirst, the longing for something that stretches beyond the horizon of our mortality—let's call it heaven, the undiscovered country—is merely nostalgia. Behold the continuation of an illusion! It used to burn bright, when the likes of Augustine and Aquinas could not only take it seriously, but invest themselves in its promise. Indeed, once upon a time even a cantankerous genius like Dante could believe in a heaven which, even though no one had actually been there, was nonetheless where each of us truly belonged—was home. You are welcomed in. You receive a white stone, which discloses your true identity: "and on the stone is written a new name that no one knows except the one who receives it" (Rev 2:17). But it is not just all about you. In paradise you discover yourself in a community where everybody knows your name, a corporate life in which each person experiences the same reality—God—but differently.

Furthermore, in heaven one could let go of the preoccupations of the past, with all their pointless ego entanglements. Who cares, for instance, if the Florence to which you gave your best turns its back on you, throws you out with nothing to call your own except the conviction that you had been done a terrible injustice? You have that certainty, which you cling to with a vengeance. You also have the undertaking of a vast poem to engage you for more than a decade. In it you "in-paradise" your own mind as you imagine a new heaven and a new earth. On this journey you invite anyone who would follow in your turbulent wake, page by page. "What amazement must have filled me," writes the poet near the end of the *Paradiso*, "when I from the human came to the divine, from time to eternity, from Florence to a people just and sane" (31.36–40). Home free.

This rhetoric is powerful, and who wouldn't want to move from madness to justice and sanity, to a better world than this one? But, again, might not all this talk of a better world, an afterlife, amount to false consolation in the face of life's disappointments—merely wishful thinking? Freud, in his famous indictment of religion, thought so; so too do the likes of Christopher Hitchens and Richard Dawkins, who have recently tried to turn back the heaven-believing fundamentalist tide with such polemics as *God Is Not Good* and *The God Illusion*.

These authors make their point in serviceable prose, but if you want to follow their argument in gold it is best to turn to the poet Wallace Stevens, with his unexcelled gift for debunking the divine. Stevens spent his poetic career asking us to imagine our evenings without angels, our Sunday mornings spent contemplating mundane life rather than courting a "tomb in Palestine" and whatever allegedly lies beyond it. Bare earth, not fantasies of some imperishable bliss, is always best. Why? Because it is real and, consequently, mortal, "[a] part of labor and a part of pain."[40] Why speculate about reunions with souls when the only company we ever really get to keep is with those, like ourselves, who are made of flesh and blood—"the heavenly fellowship/ Of men that perish and of summer morn"? We should not waste precious time practicing for eternity or learning to say goodbye to this mortal coil. Instead, our task is to wave adieu to the very notion of an afterlife. This world must always trump some other, no matter how magnificent its invention, no matter how seductive its Supreme Fiction. Let Dante rest secure in his mastery of hell, purgatory, and heaven. Nobody did the job better than he, but that imaginative work is long over and done: it is finished. The vocation of poets now is to celebrate the transitory perishing earth, at once beautiful and vulnerable:

> In a world without heaven to follow, the stops
> Would be endings, more poignant than partings,
>   profounder
> And that would be saying farewell, repeating farewell,
> Just to be there and just to behold [.]

Part of me is impressed with this line of thought. I am moved by Stevens' this-worldly drumbeat in "Waving Adieu, Adieu, Adieu" in a way that I am not, say, by Bernard of Cluny's "Jerusalem the Golden":

> Jerusalem the golden,
> with milk and honey blest,
> beneath thy contemplation
> sink heart and voice oppressed:
> I know not, oh, I know not,
> what joys await us there;
> what radiancy of glory,
> what bliss beyond compare!

This twelfth-century hymn—it's better in Latin!—is lovely to sing in church, as are the others like it that also hold out a winsome vision of radiant glory. Whenever I sing them, however, it is with a sense of bad faith, as if I am buying into a scenario that is not, in fact, my lively hope. The words feel antique, like light shed from a dead star. Yes, they cast a certain radiance in ceremony (the grander the better), but not otherwise. In this contrarian mood I find myself opting for Stevens' bare earth over a ghostly gathering of white robes—despite all the promised milk and honey, or, perhaps, because of it. Such a heaven is too rich for the blood, yet also has too little nourishment to offer. Give me the impossibly messy Jerusalem an airplane ride away, with all its noise and bitter contention, rather than some golden dream, some endless Sabbath.

But then there are other days and different moods, a spiritual back and forth that recalls a letter Emily Dickinson wrote toward the end of her life: "We both believe, and disbelieve a hundred times an Hour, which keeps Believing nimble."[41] When in the grip of faithfulness, which is my predominant mode, the humanist secularity of the naysayers seems too bare even for bare earth. There is so much more to "behold," so many more things happening on earth (let alone in heaven) than is dreamed of in such restrictive philosophies. Stevens suggests in "Waving Adieu, Adieu, Adieu" that by letting go of eternity's claptrap we can free ourselves to attend to reality without the distractions of otherworldly fantasy. Unburdened, one would be able to

> turn to
> The ever-jubilant weather, to sip
> One's cup and never to say a word,
> Or to sleep or just to lie there still,
> Just to be there, just to be beheld [.]

But what if one's cup is, if only from time to time, overflowing with a joy that cannot be fully accounted for? What if sleep is disturbed by dreams that take one elsewhere, or if beholding the beloved face of those who have died—the faces in framed photographs on your desk or bureau—convinces you that those persons are still alive, although in ways you could not begin to understand?

Perhaps memory *is* the other world. Or maybe it is the portal to a place, a "state of existence," we have not yet been.

Thoughts like this fall under the category of speculation rather than conviction: they are "what if?" conjectures rather than "I believe" affirmations. No doubt to the pious who rest easy in an inherited Zion, all I have to hold on to is vain imagination. For the disbelievers, by contrast, I am evidently stuck trying to retrieve something of value from a fantasy to which I remain tied. And how could it be otherwise given six decades marinating in Christian tradition and thirty-five years as a Dante scholar? Old habits die hard and, like it or not, the ancient stories retain their grip.

What then shall we say to this? True believers already have their reward: the angels beckon through heaven's open door, the seventy virgins await. It is to the confident disbelievers, however, that I am drawn—with a question. Since we have no idea if everything stops with our final breath except our rapid dissolution, why does it make sense to assume that it does? Clearly, life goes on. Even those who do not believe that there is anything spiritual to be distinguished from our physical being—those who look forward, so to speak, only to extinction—imagine a sequel. It may not be personal, as in the Christian insistence on the resurrection of flesh. But something carries on, as scattered atoms disperse into the universe and are "reborn" in some refiguring of energy. Apart from whatever human legacy we leave, our matter enters a world to come, even if there is no "us" in the equation, even if the river of life continues to flow without the momentary eddy that was you or me.

I wonder, too, if living without illusions—that is, without any thought of an afterlife—is interesting enough to support life in the here and now. It is supposed to be. Stevens argues that a world without heaven to follow makes everything sweeter, more poignant and urgent. But couldn't one also say the opposite: viewing the here and now as the anticipation of some other dimension can enrich the way we live by freeing us from the illusion that what seems is identical with what is? It is not necessary to view an afterlife as the greatest hits of this one, or as our world minus the tears. What if the other world were, well, *other*? What if you practiced for eternity by cultivating a sense of curiosity, a willingness to be surprised?

The enormous appeal of other-world imaginings is in part that they open up closed systems and thereby disenchant the status quo; they keep what is already known from attaining the last word on the possible. The visible sky is not, after all, the limit. Step through the wardrobe's stockpile of winter clothes and you enter C. S. Lewis's Narnia. Take refuge in a raggedy traffic circle on the outskirts of Oxford, like Will in Phillip Pullman's *His Dark Materials* trilogy, then stumble upon a row of hornbeam trees, only to discover what turns out to be one of an infinite number of other universes. Look long and hard at Florence (or anyplace where you happen to live) and discover the long-distance implications of what presently is too close at hand to see cleary. Imagine the other world as *another* world, one of many possibilities, each of which might help transform the way we live now. The point should never be to sell the credulous a false bill of goods—rather it is to open our minds to the good we are not accustomed to seeing, to love the unknown, not fear it.

Maybe the best way to treat the life of the world to come is to court it respectfully from a distance, that is, from our position of profound ignorance. Let it become an exercise in faithful imagination, a matter of "perhaps," or "what if?", or "might it not be?" If God were "all in all," then what would we find? More importantly, who would we be—and be now, not just in some life to come? Christian surmise is essentially what Augustine gives us at the end of the *City of God*. It is also what Dante practices throughout the *Paradiso*, when all the assertions of what he saw are undercut by his acknowledgment that it was more, "so much more," than what he remembers or could ever say.

Henry Ward Beecher's contemporary and biographer Lyman Abbot records that he delighted in carrying about with him a pocketful of precious stones. He "loved to watch the colors come and go in their cryptic depths as a child might"; in looking fixedly at one stone, he said he felt "as if there were a soul back of it looking through the rays of light flashing over it and in every way seed a thing of life."[42] What we have in our pockets are not uncut gems but only hints and guesses, intuitions and dreams, holy hunches at best.

Start at the threshold. Forget trying to envision eternity or an endless Sabbath, which is impossible for anyone as time-bound as we are. Instead, imagine taking a first step into the City of God. The poet of the *Paradiso* depicts a pilgrim who is wordless and abashed, as open-mouthed and gawky as someone from the sticks who takes in the wonders of Rome for the first time. Because he knows nothing he stands to discover everything, and to be blown away by it.

John Donne conjured that same step into the great beyond on May 30, 1621, when he preached at the marriage of Mistress Margaret Washington in the London church of St. Clement Danes. Wanting to find a connection between this particular occasion and larger Christian concerns, he drew an analogy between the happy couple's union and the wedding of the soul to Christ at the Lamb's High Feast. Because he was the kind of preacher who went for broke, he dared to imagine himself as the Christian soul in question, who, because of New Testament imagery, could be represented as a bride come to plight her troth forever to Christ her

Lord. One wonders what the congregation in St. Clement Danes made of this gender-bending—Dr. Donne as the bride of Christ! As the preacher paints the picture of the soul's arrival in heaven, everyone in the City of God gathers to watch her long walk down the aisle. Turning to look her way are martyrs and confessors, virgins and patriarchs, even Job and Lazarus—the whole company of the blessed. Donne has every reason to expect the worst. Surely they all know that the lady in white is a girl with a past, "pure as the driven slush," as Tallulah Bankhead had it. Certainly the congregation hearing this sermon would have remembered that the bride, formerly known as Jack Donne, was a rake about town—at least before marriage, children, poverty, and ordination settled him down. He became the greatest preacher of his day, a spellbinder before kings as well as whoever was gathered in the square outside the Cathedral of St. Paul. Yet, he did not always speak out of the clouds with an angel's voice. Nor are ostensibly holy men free from the pitfalls of temptation. Indeed, they probably stand at greater risk of a fall, pedestals being precarious places to stand.

In Donne's telling, none of this matters to Christ even if everyone else among the blessed, given their knowledge of who "she" was, is whispering, "Will this Lamb have anything to doe with *this* soule?" What happens, however, turns out to be the opposite of what was expected—which may very well be the great lesson. The afterlife will always be contrary to expectations, other than what has been anticipated or feared. In this case, the Son of God as bridegroom does not care a whit that his intended's sins once were scarlet. All the bride has to do is lose her scruples, proceed, and join in the feast to follow. And so she does, with complete confidence in the bridegroom's choice of her. Even if everyone else thinks the union is a mistake, "this Lamb shall mary me," says the preacher, "and mary me *In aeternum*, for ever."[43]

Then there is Henry Ward Beecher, also imagining the threshold between life and death. He is anxious about those nervous parishioners in Plymouth Church who are terrified to meet their Maker, living in that dread of eternity which preachers used to cultivate for the sake of the souls entrusted to them. Instead, Love bade these men and women welcome, to recall George Herbert's sublime poem, yet they were always drawing back with a sense of "dust and shame." Imagine what will happen, however, when they are actually before the Lord. Says Beecher: "It were almost enough to make one's heaven, to stand and see the first wild stirring of joy in the face, and hear the first rapturous cry as they cross the threshold, of thousands of timid Christians who lived weeping and died sighing, but who will wake to find every tear an orb, and every sigh an inspiration of God. O the wondrous joy of heaven to those who do not expect it."[44]

Frederick Buechner turned to the afterlife in his third Beecher Lecture when he asked his audience to think of those moments in fairytales—or, better, in Shakespeare's late romances—when defenses are down. The dead turn out to be alive; a statue of a falsely defamed wife in *The Winter's Tale* seems to breathe, and incredulity overtakes her wretched husband as he sees the statue of his wife become her very person: "What chisel/ Could ever yet cut breath?" In such a moment of surprise, Buechner says, we are able to catch a fleeting glimpse of joy so deep that it is "as poignant as grief." When that glimpse comes, perhaps at a miraculous reunion or at a reconciliation that by all rights should never have happened, there is a "catch of the breath," the "beat and lifting of the heart." We realize at such times that the profoundest loss has become the treasure we had despaired of ever finding. Like the road that winds down through hell, the true way that was lost becomes the path to home. "Who can say when or how it will be that something easters up out of the dimness to remind us of a time before we were born and after we will die?"[45]

Three days before anything "eastered" up out of the horror of Calvary, when Jesus' breath was agonized and there was probably no joy whatsoever in his poignant grief, the gospel writers remember that he said different things. Collectively, these sayings have been canonized as the "Seven Last Words," and often on Good Friday preachers ask us to meditate on them. Because these sayings come from a distance of two millennia they may suggest something in chiseled Roman letters or medieval Gothic script. But what if we encountered them more in the vernacular, apart from the solemn context of church and Scripture or even of the printed page—heard them as they might be heard (or spoken) by anyone of us at a deathbed? Imagine, as the door is about to crack open onto that "undiscover'd country from whose bourn/ no traveler returns"—if you were Jesus, what might *you* say? Maybe what he did. "I'm thirsty." Or, "I want you to take care of my mother." Or, "It's OK, I've forgiven you. You couldn't have known what you were doing." Or, "Don't worry, I am with you today; I always will be." Or, "I'm—done— now." Or, "*Where* is God?"

First-time students of the Bible are often dismayed to realize that there is no commonly agreed upon "last word" in the gospels, nor is there a consistent way of looking at how Jesus met his death. But isn't this precisely the way it had to be? Fully human, Jesus must have run the gamut, shuttled between radical fears over his future—"My God, my God, why have you forsaken me?"—and the assurance that on "this day," as he told one of the thieves crucified next to him, the two of them would be reunited in paradise. We need the composite witness, oscillating between belief and disbelief "a hundred times an Hour." For Mark and

Matthew, who recall only the cry of dereliction, Jesus died in despair; for John, on the other hand, he is perfectly composed even *in extremis*. He has the wherewithal to settle the affairs of his mother and closest friend. He thirsts in order to fulfill prophecy. And when at last it is time to let go, he declares that everything he had set out to do has reached its perfection. "It is finished." There are no loose ends.

The Lenten hymn, "Go, to dark Gethsemane," tells Christians to "learn of Jesus Christ to die." For those of us who follow in his way, where else would we turn? Yet among his several responses to death there will inevitably be just one that we choose as our own. My choice, the dying word that takes me where I would like to go when I approach the undiscovered country, is the one that Luke remembers to be Jesus' very last: "Father, into your hands I commend my spirit." (23:46). Note his complete lack of originality! He takes comfort in tradition, quoting from Psalm 31 when he needs the reassurance of the past:

> In you, O Lord, I seek refuge;
> do not let me ever be put to shame;
> in your righteousness deliver me.
> Incline your ear to me;
> rescue me speedily.
> Be a rock of refuge for me,
> a strong fortress to save me.
> You are indeed my rock and my fortress;
> for your name's sake lead me and guide me,
> take me out of the net that is hidden for me,
> for you are my refuge.
> Into your hand I commit my spirit;
> you have redeemed me, O Lord, faithful God.

My guess is that Luke believed Jesus recalled this psalm because, in the end, he had complete trust in a "faithful God." He was a Jew steeped in Scripture and this affirmation, no doubt learned by heart long ago, was the one he wanted to make in the end. But what if, rather than confidently recalling a text, he was whistling in the dark—an abandoned man saying words like "rock," "fortress," "deliverance," and "refuge" over and over again, as if to summon their strength when he was all alone, hoisted up into the gathering dark? In this case he quoted the psalm because, without a hope in the world, he was left with nothing else. Or was he looking beyond the apparent darkness to a light that *must* be there, radiant, just on the other side of what he could see? Maybe when he cried out, "Father, into your hands I commend my spirit," he did so as much in crazy hope as in conviction. Maybe he was taking a leap of faith without a safety net because there was nothing left to lose.

Speculations like these have no resolution. None of us were there, including, by his own testimony, Luke himself, nor can any of us put ourselves in Jesus' unique place. But this much is clear: when Jesus places himself into his Father's hands he is a world away from uttering the psalmist's other outcry, the one that Matthew and Mark report. For instead of "My God, my God, why have you forsaken me?" Luke's Jesus leaps in hope. He may be caught helpless in the enemy's net and nailed to the cross in shame, but no matter. God is a rock, a refuge, a fortress. Though skewered in the flesh, he can still take a running jump of the soul and, with a loud voice (and his last reserve of strength), whisper or shout, "Into your hands I commend my spirit." Ready or not, here I come, Father—to you. He leaps into what he hopes will be open arms, but no one can say for sure what he found after the death rattle. "The rest," as Hamlet says in *his* last words, "is silence."

In the Calvary scene described variously by all four evangelists, the dying Jesus offers no forecast or blueprint for the beyond; he bequeaths no vision. There are, of course, the post-resurrection accounts in Luke and John, with their breaking of bread and grilling of fish—but no description of the other world that awaits. This fact may serve as a warning to those who dare to go beyond where Jesus himself left off. Simply commending ourselves to God, handing ourselves over to the unknown, may be the way to go. No flights of angels singing us to our rest, no radiant door opening upon everyone we have been longing to see.

On the other hand, if such visions help us to face the unknown with joy, it is a pity not to foster them—as long as God is always acknowledged to be the final surprise, to hold the last word. Imagining the world to come allows us to try on a new world for size and, once we do, to realize that what we have come up with thus far is too constraining and small, too shopworn and hand-me-down—not wild enough. For this reason everyone derides the justifiably lampooned heavenly cloud puffs, halos, and harps. They are too tame for us, let alone for God.

But with or without harp accompaniment, singing in the company of other people may be a fruitful way to imagine heaven. Dante realized the truth of this, first in his purgatory, where the penitent souls chant psalms and hymns in unison, and then in his polyphonic paradise, where the voices of angels join those of redeemed humanity. And yet no one needs the *Divine Comedy* to recognize what music can do. Anyone who has ever sung in a choir or, for that matter, been part of a robust congregation, exuberant piano bar, or stadium sing-along knows its power.

Music can change everything. It can take over a room, leaving no one uninvolved or untouched. Even when it is scripted, paired with text, it ultimately leaves words behind and with them, thought. It takes us to resonant places inside our bodies—lungs, diaphragm, throat, skull—but also to "states of experience" that are, strictly speaking, no place at all. Mere air flowing through our flesh and bone conjures a thrilling "there" as palpable as anything else in the universe, even though we cannot touch it, even though it defies both musical analysis and psychological explanation. And there is an additional comfort: you do not have to be "good" at music to be transported by it, most especially if you experience it with others. Beatitude loves company.

I remember thinking of all of this at a performance of Bach's St. Matthew Passion. At first it struck me that each of us was listening on our own. Some were riveted throughout; others came and went with the recitatives; still others paid attention fully only during the chorales. Every audience is a motley crew. Yet at the end when it came time for applause I realized that, wherever I had been taken individually by the music, I did not go there alone. All of us were transported.

Many of the things that otherwise seem so important fade from view in such beatific moments. No matter that my knowledge of music (like my singing voice) is not exceptional, let alone trained; nor that, when it comes to music as a whole, I am definitely below the par of my friends. Many of them are professionals in one way or another; their collections of CDs and scores, libretti and concert programs climb from floor to ceiling. Take, for instance, the person sitting next to me at the St. Matthew Passion that evening—an accomplished pianist and singer as well as a European historian. Unlike him, I have no idea how Bach put these soaring St. Matthew notes together. When I asked him at the intermission if he could explain something of that magic, he did his best—patiently, as is his wont—to describe what went into the composition. I listened hard. Even though I appreciated the effort, talk of chords and triads meant very little: the how-it-is-put-together dimension of music has always eluded me. Like math, I have simply never gotten it.

As we returned to our seats after the intermission I realized that he would certainly take away from the evening's experience a far richer memory than I. In every way I came up short in comparison. Along with everything else he knew, he could compare this performance to others that he could remember in detail. He would also recall the thrill of having sung the piece more than once when he was part of the chorus. I mostly listen to CDs when I am doing something else; he, on the other hand, makes music.

Yet for whatever reason, his "more" and my "less" counted for nothing when all was said and done. What mattered was that both of us were swept away, taken someplace completely glorious by the music. My guess is that, unlike me, this happens rather often to him, but so what? That evening I too entered a dimension of meaning and beauty that I know every little about, but which I have been graced to discover, willy-nilly, from time to time. I honestly do not know what these transports mean. Trying to keep my believing nimble, I go back and forth, consider such surges of well-being to be a once-in-a-blue-moon high tide of serotonin *and* a foretaste of a world to come—or a taste of the world existing right here and now that shows itself whenever we are able to notice it.

Whatever may come—or not—it seems enough now to treasure the little bit that I can handle, the occasional moment within my ken but beyond my comprehension. Like that minute or so at the end of the St. Matthew Passion, between the roar of the applause and the fussing with coats and programs. Neither my friend nor I wanted to leave, and not only because the weather was blustery or the trolley ride home inevitably a rude climax. We wanted only to hold onto the music, stay in its light. But then, when it was time to

leave and go our separate ways, we turned to face one another—
he with a tear in his eye and me a smile from ear to ear. Not a
word was spoken but everything said. Who knows? Perhaps the
kingdom of heaven, whether it opens up now or shows itself then,
is just like *that*.

> How incomplete is speech, how weak, when set
> against my thought! And this, to what I saw
> is such—to call it little is too much.

(Par. 33.121–123)

A Due Sense
of Wonder

EPILOGUE

Before we bother to think of a world other than this one, something major has to get lost, someone important has to die. For me the bell started tolling when my Grandmother "passed away"—that was the phrase used at the time. It has continued to ring ever since, for aunts, parents, lovers, friends my own age, former students, and for a nephew and godson who was barely thirty when the Lord took his soul before he waked.

Some of these losses weigh heavier on me than others. I am burdened by unfinished business, things done or left undone: a friendship I dropped, a connection short-changed, my coldness of heart when a little warmth might have mattered. Yet whatever our parting, all of "my dead" weigh in each Sunday at the Eucharist when the congregation standing around me prays to God for the shining of light perpetual. At this time I feel the knitting together of my personal world, as intercessions for those living are joined together with the memory of those no longer here. I name the departed one by one, roughly according to the sequence of their dying: "We commend to your mercy all who have died, that your will for them may be fulfilled; and we pray that we may share with all your saints in your eternal kingdom." Some of those I name fit this commendation: it suits them. The rest will forgive me, I trust, for wishing them a godly end and a share in an eternal kingdom that did not interest them at all when they were alive.

The most recent addition to my roster is an artist and friend who died of pancreatic cancer in February 2008. Gregor and I had known one another for decades thanks to our mutual interest in religion and art, not to mention one unforgettable trip to the PTL Club's Heritage, USA at the very end of its glory days. For a number of years we had spent a week every summer working on a book in praise of the wonders of creation meant for environmentalists and Christians, people like ourselves, who were in love with the earth. She would illustrate and I would write: we would call our joint venture *A Due Sense of Wonder*.

We set up shop in July or August at her home in Sonoma, a house perched on a hillside overlooking the Valley of the Moon. Breakfast was when we talked about the upcoming day's work, lunch when we checked in on our separate activities, and the evening's *al fresco* drink (or two) when we wrapped it up. The next round began on the morrow as "evening came and morning came," another day. Although the book failed to materialize in the long run, it led us to something more significant, as such projects often do—a deep friendship based on a shared love of California, her corgis Andy and Annabella, the poet Mary Oliver, bourbon whiskey, and God. We kept track of one another's lives; we opened one another's eyes.

I was busy writing the lectures that eventually became this book during my summer visit to her in 2007, when Gregor was midway through her struggle with cancer. In the evening I would read pages from my work in progress; she would comment, and passing from my speculations on the world to come and Dante's rendition of it, we quite naturally began to discuss her death. She asked my help in composing an obituary, which brought me into the details of her life and acquainted me with achievements (artistic as well as scholarly) I had not known before. She also asked me to plan her memorial service and, when the time came, to preach at it. The liturgy would be traditional, from the Book of Common Prayer, and the trick would be to keep the service simple and welcoming. Scriptural selections were easy enough to make, but the non-biblical texts that meant most to her, and that we shared out loud in several evening readings, required more consideration. Hildegard of Bingen was a favorite but the poets Rainer Maria Rilke and Mary Oliver topped her list.

Oliver was especially compelling: her keen eye for the natural world matched Gregor's own, as did her expression of faith in God. That faith was pervasive but reticent, full of questions, long on praise. For both women revelation was rooted in what we could see and touch. It was brought into momentary focus by a flower, a bird, a deer. There were many poems to savor along these lines but the one Gregor liked best seemed to sum up the way she lived and the spirit in which she was preparing to die, "When Death Comes."[46] This poem would not be everyone's first choice for a rite of Christian burial, but it seemed to us to say what could be said, not in a liturgy—the Book of Common Prayer would take care of that—but by people like Gregor herself. It is modest, presuming no knowledge of the world to come or even strong interest in it. Instead, it concerns the way we inhabit (to quote the final two words) "this world." Oliver begins by conjuring death at its arrival, when it shows up like the steady advance of "the measles-pox," "like an iceberg between the shoulder blades." She imagines herself on the verge of being devoured by oblivion, dropped like a coin into a purse that is quickly snapped shut—a coin lost, perhaps, forever. Mortality seems to have the last word here, or does it? The poet faces the future that comes to all of us but goes on to envision herself at a doorway or on a threshold. Is this because she believes that there is another side to reality than the one on which she currently stands, or because there is simply nothing more for her to say if there is not? If there is no doorway to enter or threshold to cross, then when death comes—blackout, silence.

That possibility yields little for a poet to write about, and so she continues: "I want to step through the door," she says, "full of curiosity, wondering:/ what is it going to be like, that cottage of darkness?" If there *is* another side, she wants to cross over to it asking questions, keeping her mind and heart open. She calls the undiscovered country a "cottage of darkness." Is this a coffin, another kind of purse to snap away her coin? Or is it an antechamber, a way-station to someplace or something else?

Rather than saying one way or the other, Oliver centers her resolve—and the energy in her poem—on the world she lives in. In the face of death's coming she will look on everything with new eyes, seeing only brothers and sisters whose names, when spoken, make "a comfortable music in the mouth." She will view each life as if it were "as common as a field daisy, and as singular." Time will be one possibility to meditate upon, eternity another. Nothing will be taken for granted because every creature, no matter how small, is something "precious to the earth."

Like every *memento mori* text or image, Oliver's poem is a wake-up call. From the vantage of life's inevitable fade out, she wants us to live fully in the present without worrying about the future—to be able to say, without hesitation or regret, "all my life/ I was a bride married to amazement./ I was the bridegroom, taking the world into my arms." This wedding is the poet's version of what

John saw at the end of his apocalypse, when the new heaven and the new earth descended like a bride adorned for her husband. Yet Oliver is not interested in an end-time vision, or even in what might happen when we enter "that cottage of darkness." About the aftermath of the long term ("When the trumpet of the Lord shall sound, and time shall be no more"), who knows? So too when we breathe our last: there is no telling. Yet what falls within our purview, and what may for all we know have an eternal ripple effect, is how we live *now*—not as visitors to earth but as people who belong here; not with sighs and regrets but with curiosity, amazement, joy.

Were Augustine to read my words, or the Mary Oliver poem they summarize, he would probably be turning in his grave. The whole effort of his monumental *City of God*, after all, is to pry us loose from thinking that we belong here at all. He wants to make us believe we are visitors only, people who know like the apostle Paul that our "citizenship is in heaven." Centuries of Christian piety, from high church to low, have sounded a similar note. "This world is not my home," says the gospel song, "I'm just a-passing through./ My treasures are laid up somewhere beyond the blue./ The angels beckon me from Heaven's open door/ And I can't feel at home in this world anymore."

There are others, however, for whom the door of heaven, whatever it may prove to be, opens up from this world, from this side of the blue. Treasure is found, as in Jesus' parables, in the earth, among mustard seeds that sprout in the dirt, or like yeast mixed in with three measures of flour (Matt 13:31–33). Angels may come later, but right now, God beckons along the Atlantic Coast combed by Mary Oliver in her poetry, on the Sonoma hillside where Gregor kept her watch.

My friend ended her days in a San Francisco hospice called "Coming Home." She devoted her energy to setting her own house in order so that it could be sold to people who might love it as much as she did. There were the two dogs to keep together and to place in a good home. A former graduate student came all the way from Israel to help her finish a mosaic commission that now graces the Harvard Divinity School. She managed to do that work just in time, and when it was finished she was free to let go. She died surrounded by a close ensemble of friends, who came from different periods of her life as well as from the different places she lived. Though new to one another, they fast became a community in her company.

I got to Gregor's bedside a few hours after she died. Her body was taken from the hospice even before my plane landed, so there was no opportunity to say goodbye. I felt cheated. Nonetheless on the following day, over lunch, I heard the stories of her "passing away" from those who had been able to be with her at the end. Everyone remembered the words that had been read when she died, taken from Hildegard, St. Francis, and the psalms. There was disagreement about her final words, however. Did she ask for ice cream or express impatience with the hospital bed? It seemed strange to me that a handful of people could not reach a consensus, but perhaps (as in the gospels) there never is a single last word.

Gregor had asked me to preach at her memorial service and I made good on my promise as the gift to a friend who has crossed over to whatever is next, to the undiscovered country that awaits us all. I found that the greatest temptation for as old a friend as I was to turn my sermon into yet another remembrance. After all, I had a quarter-century's worth of memories of our teaching together, of creative projects that matched my words and her images, of sitting on the balcony of her house eating, drinking, swapping stories, lamenting the sad state of the republic, and watching the daily miracle of the sun disappearing across the

Valley of the Moon behind the western hills—each day, as she pointed out to me, to a slightly different place. Above all I wanted to say what she showed me about growing up—not about growing *old*, because (for all her eighty-two years) she never actually did that, but about growing *up*.

Gregor did this by teaching me about knowing God. She had no special revelation, of course, nor any insider knowledge. She was a Christian who knew her Bible, who had a hunger for the sacramental life of the church, and who wanted her funeral to be not only grounded in the church's tradition but also wide open to all her friends, most of whom were nourished elsewhere. She was relentless on religious bigots and hypocrites, and in general the only fools she tolerated easily were the furry, four-leggèd kind— the dogs from whom she was inseparable and the mule-eared deer she fed from the back door of her house, despite the desperate pleas of everyone (me included) to cease and desist.

Her God was infinite, the great mystery understood best by those who knew they understood nearly nothing at all—Christian mystics like Dionysius, Meister Eckhardt, and Julian of Norwich; poets like Rumi, Rilke, and Mary Oliver; and the biblical psalmist who, when not singing praises with lyre and harp, is asking where in the world God has gone off to.

When Gregor built her dream house in the Sonoma hills she designed a small room on the second story that opened onto a floor-to-ceiling window. There was space only for a rocking chair and a little side table, on which she'd have a book or two, a sketch pad, and maybe a cup of coffee. I thought of it as her prayer tower—the place where she'd spend hours thinking, designing, or just holding onto the light that was everywhere in that house. I think what prayer meant for her was paying attention, sometimes with a focus, sometimes—deliberately—without one.

In fact, she built a house that mostly paid attention, looked out-doors, with each bare window framing the natural world from one angle or another. And what did her house allow her to see? The Creator's work. A hillside thick with red-bark madrone, manza-nita, and bay trees (she taught me those names); stone outcrop-pings that were the land's idea of sculpture; the orderly cascade of a neighbor's vineyard spilling downward from the brush; a hawk high in the air, riding a thermal wind in majesty.

At the core of Gregor's religion was an overriding sense of wonder—no other word will do: wonder that there should be *something* here rather than nothing at all. She was not a person unacquainted with the night; she knew darkness, and her life-long study of political philosophy, from college onwards, was an attempt to understand what it might mean to live in accord with justice—of which there was so very little in the world, as she saw with both sorrow and anger.

But the thing about Gregor is that ultimately she went for the light, gave herself over to it—in photography and mosaics; in sculptures of colored glass that shadowed the path of a day; in the brilliance of her art history lectures; and in the way she conducted her life as "a bride married to amazement," taking the world into her arms. An intimate conversation, a raucous Halloween party, a walk with the dogs down to the winery, keep-ing in touch with friends who were distant only in terms of miles: all of this, no matter how mundane, was a potential sacrament, an opening up to grace. For such a life, and for such a friend, all I could do in the end was give thanks—thanks not only for the richness of the time we all had with her, but to the God of won-der into whose unimaginable light we at last entrusted her.

NOTES

1. Frederick Buechner, *Telling the Truth: The Gospel as Tragedy, Comedy & Fairy Tale* (San Francisco: Harper & Row, 1977), 6.

2. *Literary Criticism of Dante Alighieri*, trans. and ed. Robert S. Haller (Lincoln: University of Nebraska, 1973), 101–2.

3. All citations are based primarily on *The Divine Comedy of Dante Alighieri*, trans. Allen Mandelbaum (New York: Bantam Books, 1982).

4. Henry Vaughan, "The World," from *English Seventeenth-Century Verse*, ed. Louis L. Martz (New York: W. W. Norton & Company, 1969), 389.

5. Rick Warren, *The Purpose Driven Life: What on Earth am I Here For?* (Grand Rapids, MI.: Zondervan, 2002), 31, 28.

6. *Portrait of the Artist as a Young Man* (New York: The Viking Press, 1965), 120–23.

7. Ibid., 132–33.

8. *The Autobiography of Lyman Beecher*, cited in Debby Applegate, *The Most Famous Man in America*, 20; from Debby Applegate's *Amazon Blog* (Visited September 14, 2006).

9. *Life Thoughts, Gathered From the Extemporaneous Discourses of Henry Ward Beecher by One of His Congregation* (Boston: Phillips, Sampson and Company, 1859), 182.

10. *The Sermons of Henry Ward Beecher in Plymouth Church, Brooklyn* (New York: J. B. Ford, 1871), 102.

11. *Dante, the Critical Heritage*, ed. Michael Caesar (London and New York: Routledge, 1989), 163.

12. *Aeneid* 6. 608–614. English trans. by Robert Fitzgerald, *Virgil, The Aeneid* (New York: Random House, 1983), 181.

13. For a brilliant reading of this episode that is especially sensitive to the eucharistic imagery, see John Freccero, "Bestial Sign and the Bread of Angels," in *Dante: the Poetics of Conversion*, ed. Rachel Jacoff (Cambridge: Harvard University Press, 1986), 152–66.

14. Cited in Behr, *The New Divinity*, 113–16.

15. For the text of the three Wednesday afternoon audiences on the afterlife given by Pope John Paul II in July–August 1999, see *L'Osservatore Romano* Weekly Edition in English made available on the Eternal Word Television Network Web site, www.ewtn. com/library/PAPALDOC/JP2HEAVEN.HTM (Visited June 21, 2007).

16. "No worst, there is none," poem 65 in *Poems of Gerard Manley Hopkins*, 3rd ed. (New York and London: Oxford University Press, 1965), 106–7.

17. See Jacques LeGoff, *The Birth of Purgatory*, trans. Arthur Goldhammer (Chicago: University of Chicago Press, 1984) for the fullest single-volume treatment of the subject.

18. Cited by LeGoff, 285.

19. Q.2, Appendix 2, art. 1–2. *St. Thomas Aquinas Summa Theologia*, trans. Fathers of the English Dominican Province, 5 vols. (Allen, TX: Christian Classics, 1948 [1911]).

20. A nuanced discussion of this speech is found in Stephen J. Greenblatt's *Hamlet in Purgatory* (Princeton, NJ: Princeton University Press, 2001), 203–57.

21. Catherine of Genoa, *Treatise on Purgatory, the Dialogue,* trans. Charlotte Balfour and Helen Douglas Irvine (New York: Sheed and Ward, 1946), *Purgatory*, chap. 2.

22. *Dante, La Vita Nuova (Poems of Youth)*, trans. Barbara Reynolds (Harmondsworth, Middlesex, England: Penguin Books, 1975), 41; 99.

23. *The Figure of Beatrice: A Study in Dante* (New York: Farrar, Straus & Cudahy, 1961), 232.

24. Applegate, 291.

25. Ibid., 412.

26. The sad story of Beecher's wife Eunice—who bore him many children but never seemed to grasp his attention or affection—prompts me to recall Dante's wife, Gemma Donati. She bore him three sons and a daughter, but chose to stay in Florence during the two decades of his exile. She is never mentioned in his writings.

27. All citations, Appleton, 382.

28. Ibid., 383. The phrase "nest-hiding" comes from Beecher's novel, *Norwood*, which in addition to being the author's disquisition on love bears an uncanny parallel to his relationship to both Tiltons. See the discussion of the novel, and its place in the adultery trial, in Richard Wrightman Fox, *Trials of Intimacy: Love and Lust in the Beecher-Tilton Scandal* (Chicago: University of Chicago Press, 1999), 236–44.

29. Fascinating accounts of the trial are given by Fox and Laura Hanft Korobkin, *Criminal Conversations: Sentimentality and Nineteenth-Century Legal Stories of Adultery* (New York: Columbia University Press, 1998).

30. Letter of Henry Ward Beecher to Frank Moulton, referred to as the "Ragged Edge" letter, on February 5, 1872, reproduced by Fox, 349–351, quote on 351.

31. Frank Newport, "Americans More Likely to Believe in God Than the Devil, Heaven More Than Hell," Gallup News Service http://www.galluppoll.com/content/?ci=27877. (Visited July 31, 2007).

32. "Tammy Faye Messner on *Larry King Live*, July 20, 2007," http://www.nhne.org/NewsArticlesArchive/tabid/400/articleld/3341/Tammy-Faye-Messner-On-Larry-King-Live.aspx. (Visited 7/31/2007).

33. The quote continues, "the one who [sic] she loves and has served since childbirth." William M. Welch, "Ex-Wife of evangelist Jim Bakker dies," USA TODAY, July 20, 2007, asp.ustoday.com/community/utils/idmap/29323878.story. (Visited 7/31/2007).

34. "Hymn 623, *The Hymnal 1982* (New York: The Church Hymnal Corporation, 1985).

35. *City of God* 20.22, "The saints' knowledge of the punishment of the wicked," 943–44.

36. "Because that you are going," #1260, *The Complete Poems of Emily Dickinson*, ed. Thomas H. Johnson (Boston: Little, Brown and Company, 1960), 551–52.

37. Elizabeth Stuart Phelps, *The Gates Ajar* (Boston: Osgood & Co., 1868), 140.

38. Marilynn Robinson, *Gilead* (New York: Farrar Straus Giroux, 2004), 147, 169, 166.

39. "Prescience," *God's Silence* (New York: Alfred A. Knopf, 2006), 75:

> We speak of Heaven who have not yet accomplished
> even this, the holiness of things
> precisely as they are, and never will!

My thanks to Mark Burrows for bringing this poem to mind.

40. My citations are from "Sunday Morning," *The Collected Poems of Wallace Stevens* (New York: Alfred A. Knopf, 1965), 66–70.

41. Cited by Roger Lundin, *Emily Dickinson and the Art of Belief*, 2nd ed. (Grand Rapids, MI: Wm. B. Eerdmans, 2004), 140.

42. *Henry Ward Beecher* (Hartford, CT: American Publishing Co., 1887), 178, cited by Buechner, 88.

43. Sermon # 11, *The Sermons of John Donne*, eds. George R. Potter and Evelyn M. Simpson, 14 vols. (Berkeley, CA: University of California Press, 1957), 4: 241–255. "[This] is a mariage in that great and glorious Congregation, where all my sins shall be laid open to the eyes of all the world, where all the blessed Virgins shall see all my uncleanesse, and all the Martyrs shall see my tergiversations, and all the Confessors see my double dealings in Gods cause; where *Abraham* shall see my faithlessnesse in Gods promise; and *Job* my impatience in Gods corrections; and *Lazarus* my hardnesse of heart in distributing Gods good blessing to the poore; and those Virgins and Martyrs, and Confessors, and *Abraham*, and *Job*, and *Lazarus*, and all that Congregation, shall look upon the

Lamb and upon me, and upon one another, as though they would forbid those bannes, and say to one another, Will this Lamb have anything to doe with this soule? And yet there and then this Lamb shall mary me, and mary me *In aeternum*, for ever, which is our last circumstance."

44. *Life Thoughts*, 296–97.

45. Buechner, 97.

46. Mary Oliver, *New and Selected Poems* (Boston: Beacon, 1992), 10–11. A more explicitly devotional side to Oliver can be found in *Thirst* (Boston: Beacon Press, 2006).

BIBLIOGRAPHY

Alighieri, Dante. *The Divine Comedy of Dante Alighieri*. Trans. Allen Mandelbaum. New York: Bantam Books, 1982.

———. *Dante, La Vita Nuova (Poems of Youth)*. Trans. Barbara Reynolds. Harmondsworth, Middlesex, UK: Penguin Books, 1975.

Applegate, Debby. *The Most Famous Man in America: The Biography of Henry Ward Beecher*. New York: Doubleday, 2006.

Aquinas, Saint Thomas. *St. Thomas Aquinas Summa Theologia*. Trans. Fathers of the English Dominican Province. 5 vols. Allen, TX: Christian Classics, 1948.

Augustine, Saint. *City of God against the Pagans*. Trans. Henry Bettenson. Harmondsworth, Middlesex, UK: Penguin, 1972.

———. *Confessions*. Trans. William Watts. Loeb Classical Library. 2 vols. Cambridge, MA: Harvard University Press, 1988.

Beecher, Henry Ward. *Life Thoughts, Gathered From the Extemporaneous Discourses of Henry Ward Beecher by One of His Congregation*. Boston: Phillips, Sampson and Company, 1859.

———. *The Sermons of Henry Ward Beecher in Plymouth Church, Brooklyn*. New York: J. B. Ford, 1871.

Behr, Herman, and Paul Trench. *The New Divinity: Contributions by Henry Ward Beecher et. al.* New York: Trubner & Co., Ltd., 1929.

Bloomfield, Morton. *The Seven Deadly Sins: An Introduction to the History of a Religious Concept, with Special Reference to Medieval English Literature.* East Lansing: Michigan State College Press, 1952.

Buechner, Frederick. *Telling the Truth: The Gospel as Tragedy, Comedy, and Fairy Tale.* San Francisco: Harper & Row, 1977.

Caesar, Michael. *Dante, the Critical Heritage.* New York: Routledge, 1989.

Catherine of Genoa, Saint. *Treatise on Purgatory, the Dialogue.* Trans. Charlotte Balfour and Helen Douglas Irvine. New York: Sheed and Ward, 1946.

Cogan, Marc. *The Design in the Wax: The Structure of the "Divine Comedy" and Its Meaning.* South Bend, IN: University of Notre Dame Press, 1999.

Dickinson, Emily. *The Complete Poems of Emily Dickinson.* Ed. Thomas H. Johnson. Boston: Little, Brown and Company, 1960.

Donne, John. *The Sermons of John Donne.* Eds. George R. Potter and Evelyn M. Simpson. 14 vols. Berkeley and Los Angeles: University of California Press, 1957.

Fox, Richard Wrightman. *Trials of Intimacy: Love and Lust in the Beecher-Tilton Scandal.* Chicago: University of Chicago Press, 1999.

Freccero, John. *Dante: the Poetics of Conversion.* Ed. Rachel Jacoff. Cambridge, MA: Harvard University Press, 1986.

Gardiner, Eileen. *Visions of Heaven & Hell Before Dante.* New York: Italica Press, 1989.

Gragnolati, Manuele. *Experiencing the Afterlife: Soul and Body in Dante and Medieval Culture.* South Bend, IN: University of Notre Dame Press, 2005.

Greenblatt, Stephen. *Hamlet in Purgatory.* Princeton, NJ: Princeton University Press, 2001.

Hopkins, Gerard Manley. *Poems of Gerard Manley Hopkins*. Third ed. New York: Oxford University Press, 1965.

Joyce, James. *Portrait of the Artist as a Young Man*. New York: The Viking Press, 1965.

Korobkin, Laura Hanft. *Criminal Conversations: Sentimentality and Nineteenth-Century Legal Stories of Adultery*. New York: Columbia University Press, 1998.

LeGoff, Jacques. *The Birth of Purgatory*. Trans. Arthur Goldhammer. Chicago: University of Chicago Press, 1984.

Lundin, Roger. *Emily Dickinson and the Art of Belief*. Second ed. Grand Rapids, MI: Wm. B. Eerdmans, 2004.

McDannell, Colleen, and Bernhard Lang, eds. *Heaven: a History*. New Haven, CT: Yale University Press, 1988.

Morgan, Alison. *Dante and the Medieval Other World*. Cambridge, UK: Cambridge University Press, 1990.

Morris, Adalaide Kirby. *Wallace Stevens, Imagination and Faith*. Princeton, NJ: Princeton University Press, 1974.

Muessig, Carolyn, and Ad Putter, eds. *Envisioning Heaven in the Middle Ages*. New York: Routledge, 2007.

Newhauser, Richard, ed. *The Seven Deadly Sins: From Communities to Individuals*. Ed. Richard Newhauser. Boston: Brill, 2007.

Oliver, Mary. *New and Selected Poems*. Boston: Beacon, 1992.

———. *Thirst*. Boston: Beacon Press, 2006.

Phelps, Elizabeth Stuart. *The Gates Ajar*. Boston: Osgood & Co., 1868.

Robinson, Marilyn. *Gilead*. New York: Farrar Straus Giroux, 2004.

Russell, Jeffrey Burton. *A History of Heaven: The Singing Silence*. Princeton, NJ: Princeton University Press, 1997.

———. *Paradise Mislaid: How We Lost Heaven—and How We Can Regain It* . Oxford: Oxford University Press, 2006.

Schaff, Philip, ed. *A Select Library of the Nicene and Post-Nicene Fathers of the Christian Church.* Fourteen vols. Edinburgh, Scotland: T & T Clark; and Grand Rapids, Mich.: Wm. B. Eerdmans, 1989–1994.

Stevens, Wallace. *The Collected Poems of Wallace Stevens.* New York: Alfred A. Knopf, 1965.

Twain, Mark. *Mark Twain in Eruption.* Ed. Bernard De Voto. New York: Harper, 1940.

Virgil. *The Aeneid.* Trans. Robert Fitzgerald. New York: Random House, 1983.

Williams, Charles. *The Figure of Beatrice: A Study in Dante.* New York: Farrar, Straus & Cudahy, 1961.

Wright, Franz. *God's Silence.* New York: Alfred A. Knopf, 2006.

Zaleski, Carol, and Philip Zaleski. *The Book of Heaven: An Anthology of Writings from Ancient to Modern.* Oxford, UK: Oxford University Press, 2000.